MARK PATRICK HEDERMAN

# KISSING
# THE DARK

## CONNECTING WITH THE UNCONSCIOUS

**VERITAS**

First published 1999 by
Veritas Publications
7-8 Lower Abbey Street
Dublin 1


Copyright © Mark Patrick Hederman 1999


ISBN 1 85390 424 4

British Library Cataloguing
in Publication Data.
A catalogue record for
this book is available
from the British Library.

Cover design by Bill Bolger
Printed in the Republic of Ireland by Criterion Press Ltd, Dublin

*To the Cóiced*
*who know who they are*
*and what they mean to me.*

# CONTENTS

# INTRODUCTION

This book just happened. I did not have to do anything to make it happen except produce the words. It was as if some influential power wanted it to appear and gave it an armed escort and preferential treatment at every stage of its journey to the bookshops. I had been thinking about it for a very long time. When I was nineteen I planned to understand the world I was born into by the age of forty. From then on I would explain what I had understood. In fact, it took longer than that. I have stacks of files, shelves of notebooks, numbers of articles written here and there, all containing bits of the jig-saw as I pieced it together over the years. But suddenly I was pushed into collecting some of these for the first Ennis Conference on the Millennium: 'Are We Forgetting Something?' which was organised in October 1998. After that I received a number of invitations to speak on similar topics and eventually the shape of this book emerged. I was approached by the publishers of the Ennis Conference to write a book at exactly the same time.

The book is about Ireland, about myself and about the dark. Very little of it is my own original thought. It is what I have learned painfully and collected gratefully from minds and hearts larger than my own. Sometimes I have learned these lessons by heart, sometimes I have put them into my own words, but what I have discovered about being human is a debt I owe to people too numerous to mention. Some of these I have met through books or art works, others I have been privileged to know personally. So, my text is a tapestry of wisdom borrowed or stolen from sources I hardly recall, but which has long since become both the inspiration and the vocabulary of my own life. It is not a scholarly book. Its purpose is to share an understanding with those who will be guided by the spirit to find my meaning through these stumbling words. I have kept footnotes to a minimum. Where they occur their purpose is not to identify sources; half of each page would have to be annotated to achieve such a goal. Their purpose is to provide support for an argument I have not the time or the space to elaborate, or to point towards mines of further wisdom on the topic I have barely touched upon. Also, as conventional English still lacks gender-inclusive pronouns, the use of he/she, his, hers, etc., should be understood aas referring inclusively to both genders unless the context indicates otherwise.

The book is, I hope, optimistic even in its darkness. The century we are leaving was probably the most disturbing the planet has endured. And yet I am deeply grateful to have lived my life in the second half of it. Of the discoveries that marked its high points, access to the underground world of the unconscious was perhaps the most disorienting. Discovery of a new continent in the fourteenth century made all previous geography obsolete and forced a return to the drawing-board with all maps of the world. Satellites now circling us produce pictures each second of every square inch of the globe. There is nothing left to discover on the surface of the earth. But underneath there is a frightening world elsewhere. This is the world I am struggling with in this book.

Every country, every person, has to undertake the archaeological probe which will open up that world. Ireland, as a small, discrete, self-contained unit, can be a useful paradigm. We provide a test case. I am an Irish man born in the middle of this century; I can provide firsthand experience of our particular blend of darkness.

The Republic of Ireland as an independent entity, as a self-made manifesto, with a profile described by its constitution and its laws, almost coincides with the life of the century that incubated it. We are the whole movie in miniature, the twentieth century writ small. Our society, our psychology, could be seen as a portrait of the artist as a young psychopath. My struggle to understand the world I happened to be born into made it necessary for me to come to terms with this reality as mediated to me by the Ireland of my childhood and adulthood. Ireland grew up with me and we were shackled to each other like two prisoners.

We are neither animals nor angels, a French philosopher warns us, but those who act as angels turn into animals. Like most of our contemporaries at the beginning of this century we in Ireland refused to acknowledge the darkness that was an essential part of our human condition. Everything was a halo of light, *an claidheamh solais.* We seemed to imagine that we would be the light of the world, and everything about us from politics to religion was designed to promote and to parade this rumour of angels.

This is one of the reasons why we find ourselves in such turmoil and confusion at the end of the century with scandals and skeletons emerging from attics, closets and cellars, and through every crack in the architecture designed for the angels. The way we were educated, especially those who were to be priests or professional 'religious', was in the strait-jacket of the asparagus plant, meant to travel up the funnel towards the light where it could flower at the top. The reality of what we are, socially, psychologically, sexually, was left untended and the world of the unconscious sealed off or ignored.

One of our major tasks at present is to acknowledge and appropriate the darkness which is an integral part of what we are as human beings. Such has been part of my struggle from my earliest years. I joined a monastery as a way of concentrating upon the fundamental realities of what I am and what other beings are in the world around me or in the world beyond me. I have been given the ideal conditions in which to undertake such a study. No other person of my contemporaries could have afforded the amount of time or received the privileged opportunities that I enjoyed to allow me to achieve this goal. This book is my attempt to articulate one part of the problem. There are at least three other aspects of the total spectrum which I intend to address, but this first book deals with the most fundamental, which is the reality of what we are as human beings. Monks have the responsibility to make connections that others have neither the time nor the opportunity to make. There are some who might claim that monks are the last people in the world who can tell us about who we really are, because they are either good monks and have had no experience whatever of this reality, or they have had such experience and are therefore very bad monks. My claim would be that monks are relieved of the normal responsibilities that most others have to assume, so that they can be responsible for the connections that might otherwise be ignored.

In his book *The First Circle*, Alexander Solzenitsyn describes a 'special prison' which was a technological research establishment employing highly qualified political prisoners. This more benign concentration camp was situated in a converted country house in the outer suburbs of Moscow. His novel shows that the people living in this environment became contemplatives in a certain way. They reached the first circle of themselves. Arriving at this point requires a descent into the darkness of oneself and in such darkness we are all the same. Everybody is afraid of the dark. The account he gives of the inmates of this special prison could be a description of a monastery and an explanation of why monks have something important to share:

> The men floating in this ark were detached and their thoughts could wander unfettered. They were not hungry and not full. They were not happy and therefore not disturbed by the prospect of forfeiting happiness. Their heads were not full of trivial worries about their jobs, office intrigue or anxieties about promotion, their shoulders unbowed by cares about housing, fuel, food and clothing for their children. Love, man's age-old source of pleasure and suffering, was powerless to touch them with its agony or its expectation. Their terms of imprisonment were so long that none of them had started to think of the time when they would be released. Men of outstanding intellect, education and experience, who were normally too devoted to their families to have enough of

themselves to spare for friendship, were here wholly given over to their friends. From this ark, serenely ploughing its way through the darkness, it was easy for them to survey, as from a great height, the whole tortuous, errant flow of history; yet at the same time, like people completely immersed in it, they could see every pebble in its depths.[1]

# CHAPTER ONE

# CLIMBING INTO OUR PROPER DARK

When we talk about the dark as the underground, the unconscious, we are using a metaphor. The dark, the shadow, the night-time realm of the unconscious, represents the part of ourselves we can never reach in broad daylight as a tourist or a traveller with a guide book and map. Metaphor is the way we talk about what we don't know, what is invisible, unavailable to us, using words that describe what is ordinary or familiar. Metaphor is the language of poetry, which we can use when we come to the edge of normal discourse. When our fingers can no longer touch the walls of the place we are trying to enter, metaphors act, almost like extensions of our fingernails, as bridges to the rockface beyond our reach. That is why poetry has always been one such 'door into the dark.'

We are beginning to live in a world that has forgotten what darkness is. New York is ablaze twenty-four hours a day – 'the city that never sleeps.' On a trip to Brussels in 1980, I was collected at the airport at ten o'clock at night by an octogenarian who drove his car without headlights through the city, until stopped by a policeman. The city is so well lit at night – as is the whole country – that we hadn't noticed the night-time.

This is the reality we do have to notice. Not just the physical reality of the dark, but the psychological reality, the darkness inside each one of us. We spend much of our lives asleep. This night-time realm of our unconscious is one we have to approach in our waking state. That is what *Finnegans Wake* tries to do, become Finn again but this time awake. In other words, to get back to a mythological state while retaining consciousness.

There are a number of ways to gain access to the dark of our unconscious. The first is by being attentive to our dreams. We dream every night but we may not be conscious of it. It takes time and attention to let ourselves become aware of these dreams. They are the language of our unconscious, telling us what we refuse to tell ourselves during our daylight hours. And they are not easy to interpret. We have to learn to crack the code. Most of us are both afraid and dismissive of the dark side of ourselves. We anaesthetise ourselves with sleeping pills or alcohol. Whether we kill the dark with drugs or drink or work or entertainment or sleep, the method achieves the same result: it cuts us off from an essential aspect of our lives and ourselves.

And it is so easy to imagine that this cutting off is a good thing – that light means good and dark means bad – and to draw for ourselves an evolutionary trajectory whereby we move from the 'Dark Ages' upwards and onwards to the age of 'enlightenment.' Such momentum might even tempt us to hope that a new millennium would wipe out darkness altogether, with zero tolerance for unlit streets.

For Christians, such a bias in favour of light is supported by St John, for instance, who says that 'God is light and in Him there is no darkness at all' (1 Jn 1:5). The world that refuses this light is seen as 'darkness' and those who cut themselves off from God definitively are destined for 'outer darkness.' However, even within the Bible itself another view of darkness prevails. Darkness can signify the presence of God as much as His absence. Psalm 17 tells us that 'He made darkness his covering', and when Moses meets God on Mount Sinai, in Chapters 19 and 20 of the book of Exodus, he does so in the darkness that covered that mountain. There has always been a school of mysticism which held that access to God was through darkness, whether the dark night of the soul or the cloud of unknowing.

So, darkness is an image, used here to describe a reality that we cannot reach or articulate by other means. When we call the unconscious 'darkness', we are referring to its unknowability, its inaccessibility, its scariness, which we oppose to consciousness, nearly always portrayed as a kind of light. The unconscious is that area of ourselves which is beyond the reach of our ordinary ability to reason, outside the realm of our day-to-day activity. It is a distinct area. As such it is vast, it is strange, it is hidden. We would hardly know it was there if we did not get inklings of it, whispers, rumours. That is why we have to use images from a familiar world to express it. Darkness is one such image. Two others are 'subcontinent' and 'iceberg'.

What had been discovered as the 'unconscious' was like the European discovery of America in 1492. It was the revelation that the world we knew was only a part of the whole subterranean reality. We had to reinvent our map of the world. This new dimension made everything we had thought about the world up to that date anachronistic. We had been living on the top floor, believing our house was a bungalow, when in fact there was a vast cellar underneath and we had only now been given a key to the trap-door leading into its dark, uninvestigated depths.

The image of an iceberg captured the imagination of a whole civilisation haunted by the ghost of the *Titanic*. It is not surprising that this century began with the humiliation of science, which was the sinking of the *Titanic* on 15 April 1912, and ended with the telling of this story on cinema screens and videos, to an enthralled audience of the largest proportion of the world's population ever to sit at the feet of any storyteller since the world began. The iceberg represents the tiny triangle of consciousness peeping above the water, hiding the vast bulk of itself in the depths of the ocean.

Most of us are aware by now that this century has been for many people a hell on earth and that this hell was a human creation. It was a hell of cruelty and mayhem resulting from the incapacity of powerful people to decipher their unconscious motivations, whether in concentration camps, penal institutions, schools or families.

After the holocaust there should be no possibility of neglecting the unconscious in ourselves. We have to find out about our darkness, about the shadow side of ourselves. This is not a luxury, an optional extra. It is mandatory. Whatever is not made conscious is likely to be repeated. One of the major obstacles to dealing with this reality in an effective way is the refusal to admit that it exists at all, or the conviction that it is unnecessary to find out about it and integrate it into our psychological, our social, our educational selves.

Nor is it a question of trying to substitute one for the other, of reversing the order, transposing the equation, replacing light with darkness. It is not a question of one being good, the other bad. Either in extreme form is destructive. Sunshine without shadow creates wilderness, desert; brightness without shade is blinding; intense light is as oppressive as unrelieved darkness. No, the point I am trying to make is this: we are a hybrid reality. We are made up of both darkness and light. To date we have concentrated on one of these to the exclusion of the other. This has been to our detriment because of what the unsupervised darkness has spawned.

One of Ireland's tasks in Europe in the next century must be to remind ourselves and to remind all Europeans that we carry the dark around with us, that it is an essential part of our make-up, that we never shake it off and move onwards, that we don't become children of light, that there is no such thing as progress towards complete incandescence, that, in a memorable phrase of Herbert Butterfield, each one of us remains 'equidistant from barbarity.' And that is the way it should be. The Mexicans called the European men 'Hombre', from the shadow they cast. The word, like the word 'umbrella', comes from the Latin for 'shadow.' Our role in Europe is to remind us of that definition, that reality of the shadow which we also are. The shadow in psychological terms is used to describe that part of ourselves, or that combination of features, attitudes, impulses, instincts which we find unacceptable.

We live in Europe. Seven percent of the world's land mass and fifteen percent of its population are descendants of Europa, the goddess after whom our continent was named. We make up the peoples of Europe. Our land mass is not physically large nor are we numerically dominant. Apart from Australia we are the smallest continent. However, the influence Europe has had on the planet is gigantic and indelible. Europe has been largely responsible for the way the world is today and much of that history is the result of Europe's failure to understand, appropriate and deal with the shadow side of itself.

Apart from our own dreamtime, there is also the great reminder of this reality contained in the stories of our ancestors. The Irish have one of the greatest storehouses of such commentaries in our Celtic heritage, with a mythology that is the admiration and the envy of other tribes. But such a storehouse exists for all of us as Europeans and it is from this particular source that I want to draw.

And so I begin with the famous legend of Theseus who came to Crete and with the help of Ariadne, daughter of the king, slew the Minotaur, half-man, half-bull, who consumed boatloads of young people every year. Europa (after whom our continent was named) was the grandmother of this Minotaur. Ireland's role in Europe during the next century, to put it in a nutshell, could be to act as another Ariadne to Europe's grandchildren.

So let us examine the myth of Europe more closely. Zeus/Jupiter, father of the gods, married Europa. He came to her disguised as a white bull 'not with fiery eyes and lowered horns' one account tells us, 'but gently as if to express a mute request.' The white bull carried her off to the land which he named 'Europe' after her and there she gave birth to a son, Minos.

Minos, the son of Europa, married Pasiphae who later developed 'a monstrous passion' for a bull. The offspring of that passion was the Minotaur, 'a monster half-human half-bull' who fed exclusively on human flesh. A prison-palace was constructed for him from which no one could find an exit. They called it the Labyrinth. Here the monster fed on supplies of youths owed to Minos as tributes from neighbouring non-EU members.

Eventually that great slayer of monsters, Theseus, arrives, fresh from several exploits, including the extermination of the Pallantid nephews of his father, the tearing asunder of Sinis on sprung pine trees, the killing of Phaea, the wild sow of Crommyon, the dashing of Sciron against a boulder, and the cutting short of the criminal career of the giant Polypemon, who lay his victims on a bed and stretched them if they proved too short, or lopped off their limbs if they proved too long. More recently, Theseus had gone in search of a wild bull which was devastating Attica. He captured it near Marathon and brought it back to Athens where he sacrificed it to Apollo Delphinios. In other words, plenty of violence, plenty of death, and particularly zealous destruction of anything in the nature of a bull! We join him for our purposes here as he turns his attentions to the Minotaur, 'the monster of the dark.' He is helped by the daughter of Minos, Ariadne, who, it is sometimes forgotten, is Pasiphae's unmonstrous off-spring and sister of the Minotaur. She falls in love with Theseus and before he enters the labyrinth gives him a sword and a ball of silken thread which he ties to the entrance and which then leads him out again after he has slain the Minotaur.

In this blessed twentieth century we have begun to crack the code of these dreamlike sequences; we have revisited the labyrinth and have begun to rehabilitate the Minotaur. We have understood that gods and goddesses placed by antiquity in the heavens above or in the depths of the ocean below are to be discovered inside ourselves, deep in our own intestinal labyrinths. The bull is ourselves at our most vital, our most dangerous, our most horny. And the Minotaur is the way we have described the monstrous conjunction of these aspects of ourselves, the human, the angelic, the divine. We have reviled ourselves as Minotaurs. We have created this scapegoat for the dark side and constructed an underground labyrinth where we hide one of the most important aspects of ourselves.

European culture, and particularly Irish culture since the foundation of this state as an independent entity, has been constructed over this labyrinth, which has been closed off and sealed with impregnable hubcaps, leaving the reality below to fester unattended as in a pressure cooker. These ideals, on which we Europeans based the conduct of our lives, are hybrid and ancient, coming as they do from European philosophy at its deepest and most idiosyncratic. They are also very noble. They have inspired the philosophy of Plato, the intellectual mysticism of Plotinus, the Gothic cathedrals of Europe. But the trouble is that they are not us. We are made up of both shadow and light. We are irretrievably creatures of darkness as well as beacons of light. When this is not acknowledged, catered for, assumed and integrated into our full humanity, then we become dislocated, schizoid, two-timers. If, like Rochester in Jane Eyre, we lock up our mad wife in the attic, or in the labyrinth under the cellar, and pretend to ourselves and to everyone else that she does not exist, that she is not there, eventually she will escape, creep out at night and burn the house down.

A valid question might be why we had to wait through twenty centuries before we woke up to this reality? Some say we couldn't face it until now, that we were unprepared for such exploration until the conscious side of ourselves had developed the tools that would be necessary both to achieve the exploration and to survive it. The development of these was made possible by concentrating our energies in the direction of light and not being distracted by less manoeuverable concerns. In other words, it was only because we refused to acknowledge the existence of the unconscious that we were able to concentrate on making scientific consciousness the powerful weapon that it is today. Science, as well as providing methods and equipment, also developed attitudes of mind: there was nothing we could not know, nowhere we could not explore.

Resistance to all such entry and discovery was particularly trenchant and totalitarian towards the end of the last century and the first half of this one. In this there was little to choose between Victorian England and Catholic Ireland. In fact, all movements in society which have been classified as Jansenist, Puritan, Fundamentalist, are only exaggerated versions of most religious thought systems, all of which waged war against science as an ungodly and irreligious attempt to hijack the planet for its own atheistic purposes. And these purposes were presumed by most religions to be hedonistic if not immoral.

On the other hand, it is also true that most self-respecting scientists of the same period had to be agnostic and positivist. Religion was superstition, for which scientific explanation could be provided in terms of 'compensation', 'projection', 'opium of the people'. In such an antagonistic climate, twentieth-century Europe and North America became both the time and the place of the 'discovery' of this subcontinent of the unconscious and the locus of the reaping of its whirlwind.

Psychology was the new science which was born in such circumstances and which forced its way into the underground. Because of the atmosphere surrounding its birth, it became a brash, self-opinionated know-all, repudiating all ancestry and belittling any challengers or competitors. It made exaggerated claims for its own omnicompetence and took on all opponents aggressively. As the brood began to spawn, it was inevitable that totalitarian tendencies and sibling rivalry would cause the newly established science to splinter into antagonistic denominations.

Sigmund Freud, as one of the first and perhaps most notorious pioneers, became symbol and symptom of 'psychology' as I am presenting it here in caricatured terms in its role in the pantomime of early twentieth-century drama. When on his seventieth birthday, Freud was hailed as the 'discoverer of the unconscious', he corrected the speaker and disclaimed the title. 'The poets and philosophers before me discovered the unconscious', he said, 'What I discovered was the scientific method by which the unconscious can be studied.' Long before Freud and this century, artists had both encountered and given expression to the unconscious, sometimes in symbolic form. Moby Dick, for instance, is an American parable. Dr Jeckell and Mr Hyde are previews of what happens when the unconscious is neglected. Ordinary people become monsters overnight. The writings of the Brontës are peopled by archetypal characters from the unconscious. Heathcliff is a changeling from the dark side. Dostoyevsky's stories were hailed as prophetic descriptions of later twentieth-century history, whereas they were *Notes from the Underground* as he called them in an early novel.

And so, certain kinds of art are a way of accessing the unconscious.

Such art provides a door into the dark. This door is a lintel, a frame, a threshold, a surface with hinges, that opens onto something else. Art frames a picture. The picture can be a symbol of something sensed, experienced and expressed. It can be the hidden life of the artist, life as it flows through the minutes of a day and the porous sensitivity of the one who tries to 'grasp the living passion as it rises'. The work of art can be a relic of ungraspable, fleeting, but deeply registered experience.

Science deals with the facts that apply to all of us, the inexorable laws governing each of us as samples of the species: we all get wet if we plunge into water, we all break bones if we dive into cement, we all burn if we sit on a stove. Art presents us with the possibilities open to us as unique individuals. Scientific analysis of a seed reveals everything except the possibility of a flower. Art suggests to us the shape and fragrance of the flowers that can grow. And it follows these right back into the roots that nourish and that spread beneath the darkness of the surface. It makes us aware of what is peculiarly ourselves. Novels, poems, plays and music tell us articulately the things we were trying to say confusedly to ourselves, or they make us aware of what we had been oblivious to, even though it had been going on in the background of our lives. Not that one person's experience is ever precisely the same as another's, but it has enough echoes of our own to make us aware that something similar happened to us, and it makes us retrospectively sensitive to the texture and the repercussions.

Artist are like spies and explorers entering enemy territory or undiscovered lands. They leave coded signs, touchstones, sculpted shapes that describe both the direction and the contours of the journey. These 'objective correlatives', to use T. S. Eliot's phrase, 'nerves in patterns on a screen', help us to find, monitor and express for ourselves our own charting of the way through life.

Freud had claimed to have found a scientific method by which the unconscious could be studied. It was perhaps this 'scientific' approach that made many contemporary artists allergic to psychoanalysis. Artists who were themselves tapping into the unconscious as a major source of artistic endeavour repudiated the so-called scientific road to this reality. Rainer Maria Rilke (1875-1926) wrote in a letter: 'Among the many things that pass through my head is naturally psychoanalysis... I always have the idea that my work is really nothing but a self-treatment of this kind... My wife thinks that a sort of cowardice is frightening me away from psychoanalysis; for, as she expresses it, it would be commensurate with the 'trusting', the 'pious' side of my nature to take it upon myself, – but that is not right; it is precisely my, if one may say so, piousness which holds me back from this intervention, from this great clearing-up which Life does not do, – from this correcting of all the pages Life has hitherto written... The fact is, after the most serious reflection I have come to the conclusion that I could not allow myself the loophole of psychoanalysis unless I were really determined to start a new (if possible, uncreative) life on the other side of it, a change such as I sometimes promised myself on the completion of some of my books.'

Joyce called Freud and Jung Tweedledum and Tweedledee. However, his biographer, Richard Ellmann, suggests that such antagonism arose from the fact that he was working the same field at an artistic level as they were working at a so-called scientific one. 'I don't believe in any science,' he says, 'but my imagination grows when I read Vico as it does not grow when I read Freud or Jung.' With regard to the novel *Ulysses*, he claimed: 'I have recorded, simultaneously, what a man says, sees, thinks, and what such saying, seeing and thinking does to what you Freudians call the subconscious – but as for psychoanalysis, it's neither more nor less than blackmail.'

Whatever way we do it, whether through science or dreams or art, each of us has to discover and explore the labyrinth of the dark, the unconscious, the shadow side. Whatever reservations we may now have, we cannot deny that Freud made Europe aware of the darkness which before his time had been hidden, banished or dismissed by 'respectable' society. Peter Gay, in his monumental study, *The Bourgeois Experience: Victoria to Freud,* tells us:

The unconscious is intractable. At best, however tantalizing the traces it may leave behind, it is almost illegible to the untrained observer. But, while the assignment of rendering it legible and accessible to historical inquiry is admittedly difficult, it remains a decisive truth of history – a truth the historian ignores at his peril and to his loss – that much of the past has taken place underground, silently, eloquently.[2]

The title of this chapter, 'Climbing into Our Proper Dark', is taken from one of Seamus Heaney's poems. Its purpose is to suggest that European culture, and particularly Irish culture since the foundation of this state as an independent entity, has been overly obsessed by light as opposed to darkness. We have tried to persuade ourselves at every level that we were people of light, the *claidheamh solais*, angels in fact. Our task now is to explore the other side of our reality. Artists have always been aware of the darkness, the underground, the unconscious, and have given expression to it in ways that are powerful but which can and do remain opaque to most of us. We need more direct, more popular, more available explanations to make such hidden realities obvious. Freud played such a role. It was probably the scandals he caused by his deliberate outspokenness rather than any of the truths he was trying to articulate that made Europe more aware of the reality with which he was confronted.

Many artists have been helpful to us here. But none more so than Irish artists. Samuel Beckett explained the proliferation of poets in this country by suggesting that when you are living on the last ditch in Europe there is nothing else to do but sing. Certainly, living on an island makes one aware of both the meagreness of what is our own and the immensity of what is outside. Whatever the reason, the number and quality of Irish artists 'tackling this dark', as Anne Madden called it in an interview in 1997, is proportionately vast. It is randomly interesting to note that Tom Murphy's first play is called *A Whistle in the Dark* (1961); John McGahern's second novel is *The Dark* (1965); Seamus Heaney's third book of poetry is *A Door into the Dark* (1969); and Seamus Deane's autobiographical memoir is called *Reading in the Dark* (1997). For examining the dark there are few places better situated than Ireland. Brendan Kennelly has spent most of his artistic lifetime in this element:

> Got a job in the sewers. With
> Helmet gloves rubber clothes flashlamp
> I went down below Dublin
> From Kingsbridge into O'Connell Street,
> Flashin' me lamp in the eyes o' rats
> Diabolical as tomcats. Rats don't like light
> in their eyes.

However, artists are not enough. They are no more than ushers, pointers of the way. Art is both precise and personal at this level and in this dimension and thereby helps to introduce us to what is proper to ourselves. But then each one of us has to take up the torch and carry on down our own tunnel to the underworld.

The word 'proper' in the title of this chapter means 'belonging or relating exclusively or distinctively to'. It comes from the latin *proprius* meaning 'special' or 'one's own' and it finds its most specific form in the term 'proper name', indicating an individual person. So, my proper name as opposed to my surname (the one identifying me as one member of a family) is as personal to me as my proper dark. There is no general formula. Everyone has his or her own dark attic to climb into. There has never been one exactly like yours for any other human being. It is unavoidably and undeniably 'proper' – first person singular, present tense.

And yet, I do belong to a particular family and I was born in a particular country and so this personal dark has similarities with that experienced by other Irish people. There is also, according to C. G. Jung, a collective unconscious belonging to particular races, which makes their darkness more familiar to each other than it would be to an explorer from another tribe. The problems we have experienced in the last half-century were caused by cohabitation of two tribes, one asserting itself at the expense of the other. Each tribe must explore and become aware of its particular labyrinth, if it is to learn how to negotiate the labyrinth of others. In this book I am examining the 'proper' dark of the Roman Catholic tribe.

No tribe, tongue, people or nation can absolve itself from this essential task or refuse to make this journey, and we have fortunately been provided with some very talented sherpas and guides. So we can get help from our own artists even though we are not in any way restricted to these. When I suggest that it is Ireland's role in Europe to be at the forefront of this exploration, I am neither proposing some kind of shadowline chauvinism, nor belittling the efforts of other great European artists.

Indeed, perhaps the greatest of them all, William Shakespeare, has hardly been surpassed in his treatment of this subject. One example is *The Tempest*, reputed to be his last work. The play takes place in the symbolic setting of an island, but it represents each one of us in our own insular labyrinth. Prospero is both Shakespeare and each one of us in our artistic capacity as ruler of our own island and in search of harmony in our lives. The two strange creatures who inhabit the island with Prospero are Ariel and Caliban, the first representing 'spirit', the second representing 'flesh'. Prospero's daughter Miranda represents the new humanity that can come from climbing into this darkness. The famous quotation: 'How beauteous mankind is! O brave new world/ that has such people in it,' is hers. But this brave new world is a human world. When asked about Miranda: 'Is she a goddess?' the reply is very definitely: 'Sir, she is mortal.' Shakespeare is telling us that the new humanity, the brave new world, is not achieved by either rejecting or conquering ourselves. We have to free the Ariel in ourselves, the creative spirit, but also we have to assume the Caliban, the monster of the flesh. The whole island was Caliban's by Sycorax his mother until Prospero took it from him. Prospero imprisons him and treats him as 'a poisonous slave, got by the devil himself.' 'Filth as thou art,' Prospero addresses him, 'I have used thee with human care, and lodged thee in mine own cell, till thou didst seek to violate the honour of my child.' Eventually Prospero is led from this condemnatory stance to understand that in order to restore peace to the island, to his own territory, to his own humanity, he has to take a different attitude to what Caliban represents: 'This thing of darkness I acknowledge mine,' he confesses in the end. 'Set Caliban and his companions free/Untie the spell.' The play is a description of the journey, the voyage of life, which eventually leads us through the necessary and painful tempest of the title, to the discovery of our own reality within the island of ourselves. The play ends:

> O rejoice
> Beyond a common joy, and set it down
> with gold on lasting pillars. In one voyage
> Did Claribel her husband find at Tunis
> And Ferdinand her brother found a wife
> Where he himself was lost; Prospero his dukedom
> In a poor isle; and all of us ourselves
> When no man was his own.

# CHAPTER TWO

# MISSHAPEN GEOMETRIES

The basis for a world-view that extolled the bright side of everything to the exclusion of the dark, stemmed not, as many presume, from Christianity as such, but from Greek philosophy. All the words that we use to describe any of our world-views are Greek: politics, ethics, economy, philosophy, etc. Greek words also became the vehicle for Christianity in many of its fundamental formulations. The unwritten teachings of Jesus Christ became articulated in systems of thought that were available and apparently compatible. These were essentially Greek patterns of thought, although fed also by other sophisticated local cultures. The result was and is a very admirable and very beautiful explanation of the universe and of ourselves. However, it is dangerous and detrimental when it makes serious errors of judgement about who we are, about what is essential to our nature and what is not, and, above all, what an all-powerful and all-perfect God would or would not find acceptable about our humanity. Our invitation to become 'children of God', which is what the Incarnation was about, when translated into this local culture, became an invitation to renounce being human and to set about becoming divine, to stop being animals and to start being angels. The invitation is read as asking us to become the opposite of what we are as human beings. If 'spiritual' is interpreted in this way, it means renouncing or repudiating everything that is not spiritual, which means our nature, our flesh and, above all, our sexuality.

This, of course, could be a very different agenda from the one that Christ's Incarnation might have been offering. God's adoption of us as his children might have meant that our humanity was being vindicated and validated, that being fully human was being what God intended us to be – as one of the first Christian teachers, Irenaeus, born in 130, put it: 'The Glory of God is humanity fully alive.' It could have meant that becoming fully human would mean becoming holy.

This was hardly the understanding that developed as early as the second century after Christ's sojourn on our planet. Some of the less 'humanistic' interpretations grafted onto Christianity from the earliest times are well summarised, for example, the teachings of St Cyprian of Carthage. He was born around 210 and suffered martyrdom by public decapitation in the plain of Sextus under the emperors Valerian and Gallienus on 14 September 258. He was apparently converted to the faith as a mature man, was ordained a priest and then became bishop of Carthage in 249. He was forty-eight when he died and had been a bishop for nine years. His trial and execution, which are recounted in the so-called 'Proconsular Acts of the Martyrdom of St Cyprian', read like an adventure story for boys. The Proconsul Galerius Maximus pronounces sentence and is given the heady prophetic lines: 'Your death will be an example to those whom you have gathered into your criminal conspiracy. Your blood will uphold the law,' by which he meant the 'Gods of Rome and the rites by which they are worshipped.' When sentence had been passed the assembled brethren cried out: 'Let us be beheaded with him!', and followed him in a huge and tumultuous crowd. After the beheading, 'His body was exposed nearby to satisfy the curiosity of the pagans. During the night the body was removed by the light of wax candles and torches, and with prayer and great pomp it was brought for burial to a piece of open ground belonging to the procurator Macrobius Candidianus near the reservoirs on the Mappalian Way. A few days later the proconsul Galerius Maximus died.' The triumphalism and heroic bombast are blatant.

So this bishop becomes the example and upholder of another

kind of law, which he elaborated in his treatise on the Our Father, that prayer which was given to us as the pattern of all prayer. Not only that, but every priest and every seminarian in the Catholic Church is at present obliged to read this treatise not just once but every year of his life, because it is the second reading for the Morning Office in the Liturgy of the Hours according to the Roman Rite for the 11th week of the year from Monday to Saturday. Very few authors are given this prominence. Cyprian is followed, for instance, the following Sunday by Faustinus Luciferanus who is only given one slot to say his piece on the Trinity.

Here is the message as presented by Cyprian:

> How merciful the Lord Jesus is towards us, how abundantly kind and good! He permits us, when praying in the sight of God, to call God our Father and to be called sons of God even as Christ is Son of God.

And this is so. That is what the 'Our Father' both as prayer and as reality means. But then Cyprian takes over and begins to give us his own slant on the invitation of Jesus:

> Not one of us would dare to use that name in prayer, had not he himself allowed us to pray in that way. We must remember, then, dearest brothers, we must realize that when we call God 'Father', we ought to act like sons of God, so that as we are pleased to have God as our Father, so he will be pleased with us.
>
> We should live as temples of God so that men may see that God dwells in us. Our conduct must not be unworthy of the Spirit, but since we have set out to be spiritual and heavenly beings, let us have only spiritual and heavenly thoughts and actions. For the Lord God himself has said: 'I will glorify those who glorify me; those who despise me will be despised.'

The danger of so ambiguous a message is that it can be interpreted as renunciation of our humanity, to measure up to the sublime invitation that has been offered. Cyprian is quite clear: Our humanity is not something which is to be restored and revitalised in itself, it is only valuable insofar as it can become the container, the channel for God's holiness. 'We are not asking that God be made holy by our prayers: we are asking rather that his holiness should shine in us... Seeing that he has said himself: 'Be holy as I am holy', it is our earnest petition that we, who have been made holy in baptism, may continue in what we have begun.'

The ambiguity here rests in the idea of what it means to be holy. Is God saying to us: 'You be holy in your way as I am in mine. You be you, as I am me.' Or is He saying there is only one brand of holiness – mine. The only way you can share in this is by annihilating yourself so that my holiness can flood through you, take you over and make you into a little version of me. In this second interpretation the invitation issued through the incarnation would be that the least you can do is make yourselves as bright, shiny and respectable as possible. Renunciation is the way to achieve this. Renunciation of everything that is human makes you more and more 'divine.' Such renunciation in terms of the vows of chastity, poverty and obedience, for instance, were often described as 'white martyrdom.' Martyrdom of blood, which was red, meant giving up your life, and was the ideal way to enter the divine realm; its pale alternative was the daily doing to death of everything fleshly or bodily in you. This kind of holiness washes us whiter than white and removes us from any darkness whatsoever into His wonderful light, almost envisaged as a kind of liquid weed-killer, with a powerful brand-name, perpetually swirling and scouring our newly rotivated insides. 'You were washed and you were justified, you were sanctified in the name of the Lord Jesus Christ and in the Spirit of our God. We pray that this holiness may remain in us ... asking by day and by night that we be preserved ... in the holiness and newness of life given by his grace.'[3]

High-pitched harangue. An address to the troops. An appeal for the highest standards. Anything less is shamed out of court. After an invitation to the holy place, who would dream of wearing muddy boots, who would have the nerve to wear anything as unsightly as galoshes or waders. Not at all. Everyone will be scrubbed clean, wear stiff collars and starched shirts. And, more ominously, if you don't accept this invitation, if you don't want to conform to its requirements, well, you can look forward to punishment for eternity. Simple as that.

The false divisions that seem to have been grafted onto the Christian event can be described as human geometries, devised to formulate the comprehensive programme that early Christians believed to be based upon self-evident axioms deriving from the incarnation. Christ himself never wrote, as far as we know, except once in the sand. The only geometry (a Greek word meaning 'measurement of our world') Christ left us is that of the cross. To explain the possible distortion of this geometry, which I am suggesting might have happened through its translation into the culture of the Greeks, I shall use the language of shapes and forms in mathematics (the most natural language of our human minds) to describe three shifts of emphasis which have determined the European vector. By 'vector' I mean that reality which has both magnitude and direction and which determines the position of one point in space relative to another.

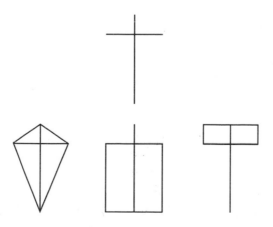

The first such geometry woven around the cross could be described as a rhombus: an oblique equilateral parallelogram, which outlines the architecture of the 'spiritual' world. The easiest way to envisage this construction is to imagine a diamond, drawn from the top of the cross to each of the arms and from each of the arms to the base. In this perception the point of incarnation is achieved with minimum insertion into the world. There is no penetration downwards from the point at the foot of the cross. Everything below this point is Hades or hell or the labyrinth of the Minotaur. All the work of salvation is filtering those who are suctioned into the space created by the immortal diamond of the cross upwards towards eternity: the unity, beauty, goodness and truth of the one true God, source and fulfilment of all that is. This cross casts no shadow, in fact all such geometries are two dimensional. The great theological syntheses of the Middle Ages were built upon this harmonius architecture, with Plato's famous line dividing the world of matter from the world of spirit, a line that travelled across the equator on the surface of the earth, and through the midriff of the human body, as the diameter of the diamond. The Gothic spires that dotted Europe are architectural symbols of the vector, derived from such geometry. The essential rhythm of this architecture is that everything comes from one and returns to one. Everything that is, is a singular substance. We stand alone. The originating principle of this world, this architecture, this humanity, is the paragon of self-subsisting, self-sufficient, self-reliant aloneness.

The second division can be described as a parallelogram of forces. It describes two perpendicular cubes on each side of the vertical cross, one on the left and one on the right, into which have been squeezed, as into two contradictory opposite compartments, the male and the female, the masculine and the feminine, Adam and Eve, Bonnie and Clyde, Samson and Delilah, Díarmuid and Gráinne, Hansel and Gretel, Frankie and Johnny, Tristan and Isolde, Romeo and Juliet, Franny and Zooey – we have created a whole alphabet of such contradistinction. Because, the laws of mathematics inform us: if two forces acting at a point are represented in magnitude and direction by two sides of a parallelogram meeting at that point, then their resultant is represented by the diagonal drawn from that point. They become diametrically opposed. But it need not be so. Things could have been different. Was this meant to be the way forward from what we read of Jesus and Mary, Jesus and the woman at the well, Jesus and Veronica, Jesus and Mary Magdalene?

Finally, if we were to form a rectangle on the top part of the cross, joining the upper arms to the uppermost vertex and declare that everything good, true, bright, white, eternal, valuable, redeemed and saved is to be found within that space and that everything outside that is bad, false, dark, black, perishable, damned and useless, we would get some inkling of the third false division which circled around the newborn Christianity.

Such mistaken divisions, which have caused our present schizoid culture, promoted the great divide between spirit and flesh, between soul and body, between mind and matter, between heaven and earth. Such a topography has obsessed the European mind from the beginnings of European philosophy and, although the paradigms have differed and the variations changed according to local and temporal fashion, the essential structures have remained in place.

The way you imagine you are determines the way you decide to behave. When you believe that the mind is the all-important element in your make-up then you try to arrange for this one element to govern the rest. You install a monarchy and your life becomes a game of monopoly. In this regard it has been constantly stated that the head should rule the heart, that reason must govern the passions, that the soul must reign supreme over the body. Various strategies have been devised to effect this monopoly and implement this policy.

While it is true that all education must in some way succeed in controlling the untamed urges of each individual – otherwise we inevitably invite a situation of anarchy and violence – the mistake here is not just that mind or spirit or soul should have the authority and the power to enslave or even destroy, but that any particular faculty or element of our make-up should be valorised and promoted to the detriment or destruction of any other. This all-powerful hegemony of a dictatorial principle over all the rest was a choice that was governed by prevailing tendencies in the cultures from which it sprang, and was decisive in, and detrimental to, the future development of European social and psychological history. It is the colonial mentality, the basis of ethnic cleansing, the carte blanche to kill whatever refuses to submit. In this despotism it is not just the choice of absolute ruler that is wrong, it is the fact of despotism itself. In other words, to trace all that we are back to one or other instinctual urge, whether this be towards sex, power or money is not simply wrong because it points to the wrong suspect on the identification parade, it is wrong because it seeks to reduce our multifaceted and variegated network of desires to one most basic one. It is the tendency to trace everything back to a single Adam or a single Eve, when the reality is pluriform and multiple. There is never just one reason for doing anything, there are usually many.

All geometry is a caricature and so are these descriptive shapes and forms. But they give us a picture of the vector created by the directive force of such ideals, which we in Ireland, as inheritors of several different cultures and a somewhat oppressive history, have allowed ourselves to perpetrate or have imposed upon us: between, for instance, the masculine and the feminine, between the head and the heart, and between the individual and the community.

The geometry of 'angelism', which produces a schizoid culture, builds itself out of the great divide between spirit and flesh, soul and body, mind and matter, heaven and earth. Something in the Irish temperament, something about our geographical isolation, something about our historical circumstances, caused a symbiotic alignment between the newly emerging Irish Republic and such angelic idealism. It was a conspiracy of wishful thinking and desire to control an otherwise irrepressible reality. It is the almost irresistible temptation of fascism when faced with the alternative of anarchy. It demands order, hierarchy, central goverment. It arranges everything according to its own categories of superiority. Everything must lead step-by-step to the highest point, which must be singular and from which must flow all legitimation and authority. The one point that remains is invested with totalitarian power over all the others.

An alternative model of authority and regulation could be found in conciliarity and consensus. Here, unanimity might be achieved by dint of understanding between, and fulfilment of, each part of the composite whole in accordance with the aspiration and identity of each. This would achieve the well-being of the whole because of the satisfactory development of each particular part. Such is the effective government of an orchestra or choir, for instance. It is government that respects individuality and originality and has the imagination and the patience to see how these can combine to produce an unanticipated harmony. It does not sacrifice idiosyncrasy and peculiarity to expediency and efficiency. It lets the flowers grow before it arranges the pattern of the garden, rather than lopping off, or weeding out, whatever fails to conform to preordained size, shape or colour co-ordination.

The way we behave is what we call our ethics. An ethics based on the geometrics we have described must inevitably prove inadequate. It proposes a morality that fails to comprehend what we are as human beings. It neither asks nor answers the right questions. When it allows some of the questions to be asked, then it might begin to move towards satisfactory and comprehensive answers that people would recognise as viable and life-promoting. Such a morality must cease to be an 'asceticism of punitive discipline' and become what Charles Davis has called 'the asceticism of achieved spontaneity.'[4]

Asceticism of achieved spontaneity is a discipline and control that emerges from a situation where each participating element recognizes the advantage to be gained and the benefits that will accrue from doing certain things in a certain way, refraining from doing others, and helping the totality of which each is a part, in order to achieve some goal or accomplish some feat. Such might be the discipline of athletes or musicians, for instance, as opposed to that of armies or prisons. Control of any kind, whether over others or over ourselves, can mirror either model. Any effective, and especially any Christian, asceticism should be based on the model of achieved spontaneity because we are convinced that it will release in us a life that is more abundant.

When we know the kind of people we were meant to be, we can summon up the courage and exercise the discipline necessary to achieve such a goal. As Kierkegaard says, when I get to the next world I won't be asked why I was not more like Christ or anyone else, I will be asked why I was not more like myself. No one minds renunciation that promotes life, that cuts off whatever is holding us back. Renunciation as pruning. It is renunciation as punishment or as doing to death some essential part of oneself that is unacceptable. Renunciation of food, of pleasure, of even life itself, all these are possible; but renunciation of what one is, is absurdity.

No morality that forbids us even to enter the attic and examine our proper darkness can be taken seriously in present circumstances. This century has been the victim of too many people who were afraid to spring-clean this attic, who refused to face the darkness, or who dogmatically declared that there was no such reality as the unconscious. Their own darkness came out in spite of themselves, and our century is scarred by the havoc then wrought. But that is historical evidence on a grand scale. Every individual life is also tainted by the leakages from an unexamined and inadequately housed shadow side.

# CHAPTER THREE

# RHOMBOIDAL REMOULDS

Several basic options of Western civilisation, mostly Greek in origin, but reinforced by a certain understanding of Judeo-Christianity, have supplied the geometry from which we have built the twentieth-century labyrinth of our Western European lives. The establishment of one principle as the focal point or centre from which the unity of all the rest would derive became an overriding obsession. It was a geometry of domination by which 'the one' ruled 'the many', 'the same' colonized 'the other' and 'spirit' held sway over 'matter', the mind over the body. This idiom of centralised domination became universal currency at most levels of human endeavour, whether psychological, ethical or political. Rationalism, the hegemony of mind over matter, was its psychological manifesto. Imperialism, or the colonial conquest of the 'uncivilised', was its translation into politics. Self-conquest, or the suppression of unruly impulses which did not conform to the required standards, was its trade mark in the ethical sphere.

A distorted simplification of the complexity of humanity, an arbitrary selection of certain elements for cultivation and certain others for cauterisation, and the imposed authority of one particular faculty over all the rest – these provided the groundwork for the socio-cultural and psychological labyrinth that became our European heritage at the beginning of this century.

The rhomboid is the mould for two kinds of filtering which were necessary to conform to the prescriptions of this cultural option. The first is the process of abstraction, whereby everything that is, is required to present itself at the court of the human mind. To achieve this, all things outside the mind have to divest themselves of their material reality and assume the ghostly form of a skeleton, or the texture of an X-ray photograph, so they can be processed by the non-material website of the mind. Such translation of the world into the comprehensible language of the mind is a reductive process which forfeits all the sensual bodiliness of colour, surface, weight, texture, aura, oddity. All of these are ground into accessible units that the mind can digest. Unless we are aware of the impoverished version being flashed on to our mindscreens, and can make the necessary adjustment to supplement and compensate for lost quality of perception, we are likely to mistake the cartoon for the reality, the technical drawing for the house itself.

In a similar way, but at an even more debilitating level, the rhomboid can describe the kind of filtering process that was understood to be necessary to make the human reality acceptable in the divine presence. This process of spiritualisation required ascetic practices which mortified (meaning: 'do to death') the flesh, subdued the body, renounced human nature. Forms of torture were devised to achieve this goal, but the basic idea was to release the spirit or the soul from the crass material dough in which it was enmeshed, so that it could transfigure the body divested of all sinfulness, materiality, human emotion or sentiment, and present it as an acceptable offering in the untarnished precincts of the spiritual realm.

It was a lonely journey of self-sacrifice. The individual person gradually pared himself down to the quick, divesting himself of all earthly attachments, until he eventually bled back into the soul of himself where he could rise like a helium-filled balloon to the throne of the most high. The important thing was to cut oneself off from all human affection and attachment, to kill off conscientiously any natural urges of the body so that the new kind of heavenly fuel – supernatural grace – might flow through the human infrastructure. One tried to be solitary, chaste, pure. One shunned all earthly goods and material wealth. Above all one fought against one's own taste, impulses, inclinations and will.

Ireland has been represented to both itself and the world as a light to the nations, and its citizens as zealous missionaries of the angelic nature of humanity. Our more recent 'official' culture has been overly obsessed by light as opposed to darkness. Self-sacrificing zealots have been our inspiration from the beginning of our journey as a light-house off the coast of Europe. Whether they were fighting for our freedom from the tyranny of political power, or freedom from the 'flesh', they all had the same characteristics. They were hard, upright, detached, intransigent and solitary. This was the ideal. This was what one aimed for and dreamed of even if one fell short. And presumably – and hopefully – most fell short. Because successful realisation of the ideal must have meant a lonely, uninhabited existence rather like the one so vividly and depressingly portrayed by John McGahern in the character of the father in his novel *Amongst Women*.

Ireland was kept in the dark about the darkness. We were not the only population to have been consciously sheltered in this way by well-meaning authorities of one kind or another. But suppression of the darkness and unawareness of the unconscious, avoidance of all entrances to the underground, were helped by our being an island and by the cultural isolation which this made possible.

In 1937 the De Valera Constitution of our 'free' state expressed this derived philosophy in no uncertain terms. In a radio broadcast to the United States on 15 June that same year, De Valera called it 'the spiritual and cultural embodiment of the Irish people', and to mark its first anniversary in 1938, he reminded us, almost as in a sermon: 'As faith without good works is dead, so must we expect our Constitution to be if we are content to leave it merely as an idle statement of principles in which we profess belief but have not the will to put into practice.'[5] Sean O'Faolain described De Valera's philosophy of life interestingly, though unfairly, as 'something so dismal that beside it the Trappist Rule of Mount Melleray is a Babylonian orgy.'

Two years before that, in 1936, my mother came over to Ireland on the Cunard Line from America. Everybody in America knew that Edward VIII, King of England, was having an affair with Mrs Wallace Simpson. It was all over the newspapers, with photographs of the pair. In Ireland, and indeed England, when my mother arrived, nobody knew about it. It was a secret. The government had forbidden the press to publish this news; it was considered dangerous to national security, and the press obeyed. When my mother began to tell people at parties in Dublin, they thought she was off her head. Being a conscientious Catholic she asked a Jesuit priest whether it was libel, detraction or scandal to be spreading news that was common knowledge in America but completely unknown over here. 'I'm not quite sure which it is', he said, 'but it's very interesting. Tell me more.' He wanted a good story to dine out on. Gossip and scandal in Ireland were whispered from ear to ear in the 1930s, not issued in banner headlines in the daily press. In those days it was possible to keep people living on islands in the dark.

Although radio was first transmitted in 1926 and more fully so after 1930, when the booster in Athlone made it available throughout the countryside, it would have to be acknowledged that for many people in Ireland, the first glimpses they got of the door into the dark was through Gay Byrne's *Late Late Show* from the 1960s onwards.

The labyrinth established by our family and religious traditions was reinforced and extended by our educational system, which remoulded our youth in the image of the rhomboid. Martin Buber, the influential Jewish philosopher and educationist, claims that the three basic instincts detected in us from the beginning of this century, and championed by the three philosophers, Nietzsche, Freud and Marx – namely, will to power, sex and desire for possessions – are incomplete as a list. Equally primary, he suggests, is the instinct towards communion.

The fundamental option open to each one of us is whether to become an individual or a person. Put very simply, the difference between the two is this: as individuals we inhabit the island of ourselves as lonely self-contained proprietors, walling off the edges and fencing in the boundaries; as persons we come out of ourselves and inhabit the space between us and other people. This is a fundamental difference. It is also a matter of education. Education to the first option is one that cultivates in each of us what Buber calls 'the instinct of origination': we are taught to be master of our own world, instigator of all our projects, lonely inventors of our own lives. Education towards personhood as opposed to individuality means educating, encouraging, developing what Buber calls 'the instinct for communion:'

> There are two forms, indispensable for the building of true human life, to which the originative instinct, left to itself, does not lead and cannot lead: to sharing in an undertaking and to entering into mutuality... As an originator, man is solitary. He stands wholly without bonds in the echoing hall of his deeds. Nor can it help him to leave his solitariness that his achievement is received enthusiastically by the many... Only if someone grasps his hand not as a 'creator' but as a fellow creature lost in the world, to be his comrade or friend or lover beyond the arts, does he have an awareness and a share of mutuality. An education based only on the training of the instinct of origination would prepare a new human solitariness which would be the most painful of all.'[6]

This is precisely the kind of training and education that Europe has given her children, and that we have continued to give our children since the foundation of the State. The points system, for instance, is designed to create that 'new kind of loneliness.' Not enough effort is made to develop or to train the instinct towards communion, the relational capacities of the young. The amount of information that each child is required to assimilate, the impersonal settings that make such distribution of information to the masses of children economically possible, and the passive receptivity required to make such transmission effective within the short time of compulsory schooling, all conspire to eliminate the possibility of growth in another direction.

This one-sided orientation is camouflaged by the apparent success of the present system in providing employment. However, for those who are unemployed this system can only instil guilt and purposelessness when the goals for which children have been prepared exclusively are unavailable or unattainable. The concomitant inevitability of frustration, drug addiction, alcoholism, vandalism and lawlessness point towards the failure of the system to cater for whole aspects of integrated growth. In fact our whole student population is undernourished in the emotional and relational aspects of their lives. There has been little attempt to explain, to train, to encourage or to mature the relational, emotional or sexual life of our young people. It was as if such life did not exist, or needed no training, direction, understanding. Or else it was presumed that it arrived fully-fledged and mature in the marriage bed, which was the only location where practice of its genital exercise was permitted. Even the most basic courses and videos on love-making teach that a man has to train himself to prevent orgasm occurring prematurely before it can be shared with his partner. This does not come naturally. On the contrary, the natural orgasm and ejection of sperm for a man is unencumbered and immediate. That is the biological way, the optimum performance in terms of procreation and reproduction of the species. But in order to humanise that instinct and introduce its relational dimension, causing tenderness, mutuality and reciprocity to imbue it with their celebrated meaning, people have to be told, have to listen, have to be humble apprentices to love, have to learn, discipline themselves and gain a control that will help them to be sensitively reciprocal in their sexuality. Otherwise sexuality is the tool of selfish individuality and autistic monologue.

If that is true for married couples, it is even more so for the trainees of perfection, the initiates to priesthood and the religious life. We could multiply by a thousand such insensitivity and ill-preparedness when describing the education provided for those shining examples of the 'angelic' life, our priests: so many well-meaning and innocent young people who entered the labyrinth of the seminary.

Stories are told by benumbed, bewildered, browbeaten seminarians of how they were required to kneel in white surplices holding lighted candles while the treatise on chastity was read to them, the high ideal that was meant to be their goal. Of how, when awkward stirrings of the 'flesh' occurred, and they believed that God was withdrawing their 'vocation,' they were told to take a cold bath, engage in energetic physical work or sport, and pray to Our Lady.

If there is any truth in Freud's description of the development and growth of sexuality then two things are clear: without positive and enlightened education, this vital aspect of ourselves can be arrested at a certain stage and cause neurotic behaviour, but with enlightened education it can become subordinated to goals other than the reproductive function:

> Sexual life does not emerge as something ready-made and does not even develop further in its own likeness, but passes through a series of successive phases which do not resemble one another; its development is thus several times repeated – like that of a caterpillar into a butterfly. The turning-point of this development is the subordination of all the component sexual instincts under the primacy of the genitals and along with this the subjection of sexuality to the reproductive function. This is preceded by a sexual life that might be described as distracted – the independent activity of the

43

different component instincts striving for organ-pleasure. This anarchy is mitigated by abortive beginnings of 'pregenital' organizations – a sadistic-anal phase preceded by an oral one, which is perhaps the most primitive. In addition there are the various, still incompletely known, processes which lead one stage of organization over to the subsequent and next higher one.[7]

Whether or not we agree with everything Freud says, it seems plausibly verifiable to me that the understanding, education and development of sexuality follows a pattern. We are sexual all our lives. 'To suppose' Freud says, 'that children have no sexual life ... but suddenly acquire it between the ages of twelve and fourteen' is as 'improbable and senseless biologically as to suppose that they brought no genitals with them into the world and only grew them at the time of puberty.' What does happen at puberty is the awakening of the 'reproductive function.' When this happens, Freud continues, 'it makes use for its purposes of physical and mental material already present.' This means, as he also points out, that the child is bound to have a perverse kind of sexual life because the organs that are meant to provide the adequate channels for the reproductive function have not yet grown sufficiently nor are they effectively connected to the eventually genitally oriented biological system.

Three things become obvious for a society that has consistently refused to face up to the reality and implications of universally transmitted sexuality:

1. There are some whose 'reproductive function' remains dormant and may not wake up until they are much older, if at all. Their sexual life remains pre-pubertal. This means that their sexuality lurks in the background and seeps into areas of attitude and behaviour of which they may well be innocent or unconscious. Some young people who entered religious life at a very early age, or remained in a protected environment during their lives, can

remain such sleeping beauties for a very long time. Some may have taken vows of chastity, which increase the possibility of remaining asleep as effectively as sleeping pills. This was the probability which so enraged Nietzsche. He thought that the possibility of being anaesthetised for life was the ultimate blasphemy. However, he saw another, more dangerous eventuality: that the dormant sexual life would have a sleepwalking existence of its own. It would appear and make its presence felt even if the sleeper was unaware of it:

> With some, chastity is a virtue, but with many it is almost a vice. These people abstain, it is true: but the bitch Sensuality glares enviously out of all they do. This restless beast follows them even into the heights of their virtue and the depths of their cold spirit. And how nicely the bitch Sensuality knows how to beg for a piece of spirit when a piece of flesh is denied her.

2) At a much later stage than is normal for human beings, somebody either accidentally or intentionally awakens the sleeping beauty and, as Ingmar Bergman so hilariously describes in his biography *The Magic Lantern*, opens the prison bars and lets out a raving lunatic.

3) Instead of recognizing this retardation or the arrested development that causes them to remain in an anarchic state of sexual panic, they pursue whatever happens to appeal to them in the way one might continue to read comics, eat baby-food or inhabit *Dempsey's Den*.

At the other end of the sexual spectrum, then, is the possibility of becoming that kind of sexual being that relates to God. The bodily reality here concerns relational energy. This normally moves from the centre to the periphery of the person, from the heart to the skin, and expels itself outwards towards the other person in the movement of orgasm, if channelled through the sexual department. However, it can be contained and redirected in a way that processes it differently. A man who is sexually active is habitually directed towards and committed to the achievement of orgasm at least every three days. His body is then attuned to the recreation of this possibility by the refurbishing within himself of the testosterone expended in the previous orgasm. If one trains oneself to interrupt this cycle and to prevent its repetitiveness in carrying on this habitual and compulsive search, the need for such gratification decreases and the energy finds another direction. This has been identified, experienced and ratified in many religious traditions. This transformation can mean coaxing the organism to make a further change, as in the caterpillar to the butterfly image. Every religion that seriously proposes full-time contemplation as a way of life has identified celibacy as the appropriate way of redirecting energy in the direction of the divine. This happens when that energy is focused upon and directed towards the base of the spine and allowed to travel upwards to the area of the brain. Meditation techniques of various kinds, involving posture and concentration and, as in tantric religion, exercises in sexual continence, which include sexual intercourse without reaching orgasm, have been devised the world over to help lovers of God to become in this way 'theosexual.' Just as it is possible for athletes and astronauts to train themselves to make their bodies perform in a way, to an extent and in a particular direction that seems impossible and unnatural, so those who freely choose to love in this way can focus themselves in the direction of the divine in a way that changes their total orientation.

Recent studies in neurobiology have suggested that the human brain at its highest point is not so much a definite structure in itself as a kind of plasticity awaiting the arrangement that the particular person wishes to impress upon it as the appropriate receptacle for the kind of life one wishes to lead and the kind of person one decides to become.

I believe in the possibility of celibacy and the condition of Christian chastity as fullfilling ways of being in relationship with each other and with God, but I don't believe that they happen at this side of the threshold of sexuality, nor do I believe that everyone who wants to devote his or her life to God should be required to be celibate. These are very particular ways of being that require not just understanding and training, but a desire and a capacity to follow them as a way of life. The fact that relationship is connected to sexuality in some way, and that all energy is one, yet can be channelled into different organs of expression, has been the reason why contemplatives in every religious tradition have always associated celibacy with the most sublime connection to God.

# CHAPTER FOUR

# PARALLELOGRAM OF FORCES

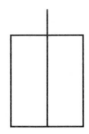

Myths and legends are to peoples what dreams are to individuals: a reservoir of enigmatic, cryptic accounts of how we have tried to come to terms with the world we have found ourselves in. They can be read horizontally as a story, or vertically as a suggestive concatenation of images. As in the legend of the Minotaur, several different civilisations have taken the basic stories of peoples they invaded or annexed and have put their particular twist to the tale. But whatever the twist, the tale has always been the tale of a bull. There is an obsession with the bull, which has represented for our ancestors something akin to the horned embodiment of vitality, the male form of the lunar goddess, whose ritual slaying was a fertility rite, ensuring the resurgence of springtime by propitiatory sacrifice to the dark phases of the moon.

Mythology, at one level, tells stories that are remnants of ancient, pre-literate, cultic ceremonies of worship of the sun and the moon. These myths represent 'a cycle of sacred marriages between the sun as the bull and the moon as the princess or priestess.' All the female names in our opening myth of Theseus, Ariadne and the Minotaur refer in some way to the moon, as the male names do to the sun. 'This essential relationship between the masculine and feminine modes of being is perhaps the most fundamental aspect of what is being explored through the stories of goddesses and gods.' Symbolically, then, Theseus becomes a figure of the archetypal masculine, whereas Ariadne represents the archetypal feminine. Her name was originally Ariagne meaning 'holy and pure', a superlative form of Hagne, which was Persephone's title as queen of the underworld, from which our word 'hag' is derived.[8]

The second superimposed geometry, which I am suggesting was nailed to the cross, caused too categorical and unequivocal a divide between male and female. This is not simply the well-rehearsed disparity and inequality between men and women as individuals and genders, but also that between the masculine and feminine principles which make up each one of us.

I do not know whether there was ever in the past a culture that was less patriarchal, aggressive, and war-loving than our European culture has been and still is. It is almost as if the cross was taken out of the ground and wielded as a sword. We only have to look around us today to agree that the power of the sword, or its contemporary substitute in tanks and war planes, is the dominant motif of our culture. There are those who would claim that some aboriginal cultures, even our own ancient Celtic culture, were less violent, less misogynistic, less power-lusting. I have no idea and I somehow doubt it. I imagine it was a question of quantity rather than quality, of less rather than unlike. It was just that Niall of the Nine Hostages didn't have nuclear warheads.

However, whether there was or there wasn't some golden age in the past, there is no reason why we should not try to create one for ourselves at this time, at any time. No reason, that is, other than the reluctance and unwillingness of some human beings like ourselves, of some part of every human being like myself, to implement it. The first step towards weaving such a culture is to accomplish it in ourselves. Because culture is a thing we weave ourselves.

We are 'unfinished' animals who complete ourselves through culture. There is a difference between the evolutionary process that unfolded the animal, vegetable and mineral world, and the world that is now in place since humanity established itself and became the dominant species on the planet. Animals are determined by nature. They do nothing more than instinctively fulfil the pattern inscribed in their genes and chromosomes. They are DNA docile. Our DNA only provides us with a Lego set to build our own completion. Ours is not a blueprint encoded in our genes, it is the basic score for an unfinished symphony. We complete or finish ourselves through culture. We are what Cifford Geertz has called 'cultural artifacts'. We become who we are 'under the guidance of cultural patterns, historically created systems of meaning in terms of which we give form, order, point and direction to our lives.'

So, if we can choose to develop a more balanced and humane culture than the one we have inherited, we should not wait another minute. We should begin to do so. And beginning means searching for other models, alternative paradigms, because it is difficult to create a whole system out of nothing and, in terms of human development and tradition, there is always wisdom to be gained from the lived experience of the past.

That is why we return to art and literature to find the recorded experience of our ancestors – the way they coped with their surroundings and created the delicate canopy that covered their nakedness which, once established, became known as their culture. Study of such art reveals a wealth of imagery and imaginative symbolism. However, there are two dominant motifs that separate most of these cultures into strikingly alternative view-points. The chalice or the cup on the one hand, and the sword or the blade on the other.

The first is a culture that cherishes fertility, growth, variety, abundance, the second is a culture imposed by order, discipline, domination, uniformity. Feminists have suggested that the emblem of the first is a woman giving birth, that the emblem of the second is a man dying on a cross.[9] There is no doubt that European culture, from the Roman Empire to the two world wars of our century, has been a culture dominated by the sword.

When we propose to challenge such a culture and work towards another paradigm, we do have examples of cultures that were built on the archetype of the chalice or the cup as an important precedent and an encouraging alternative. Religion, being one of the most important instigators and preservers of any culture, supports and perpetuates the social organisation it reflects. Most Indo-European religions regarded weapons as sacred properties of the Gods. The glorification of the blade, the sacred sword or dagger, and the resultant organised slaughter of propitiatory victims, was a natural worship of a pantheon of Gods as bloodthirsty as they were bellicose. The religious mythologies, the manifest destinies of history, that gave divine mandate to all kinds of ethnic cleansing, crusades, inquisitions, world wars, religious wars, provided absolute authority for an arms race that has allowed us to achieve a technology of destruction, the like of which, in the past, was attributed only to the wrathful Godhead alone, and which puts in the hands of individual people the future of all life on the planet. This is both the product and paradigm of European culture as we have created it and as we have been created by it.

There have been other cultures, other models, alternative paradigms. Neolithic art, which emphasises the chalice, the cup of salvation, and its later manifestation in Minoan art, in Crete, which we might call Old European culture, seem to express the view that the mysterious power or powers that govern the universe are more interested in abundance of growth, in generous fertility, in manifold creativity, than in destruction, desolation and dire punishments for disobedience. Weapons are unknown as religious images or symbolism. The snake and the butterfly replace the sword and the dagger as representations of metamorphosis and regeneration. The butterfly is symbol of transformation to another kind of existence from the earthbound one of the caterpillar. The snake shedding its skin is revitalising itself and starting anew. This figure is also present in its more abstract form of the spiral and the labyrinth. The cult of the bull and the famous labyrinth of the Minotaur are forms of a more ancient religion which cherished the life-giving forces and sacred fertility of the earth, as nurturer and provider of that cornucopia, the horn of plenty, which was the centre of all cultures of the chalice and the cup.

There is a great difference between biological evolution and cultural evolution. In the first case, the planet becomes the theatre in which instinctively and mechanically the life force emerges in the widest possible variety of progressively more complex forms. These compete and survive to the extent that they are strong enough, or adaptable to the conditions that exist around them. The miracle is that in such a race for the survival of the fittest, our own ill-equipped and fragile species should have made it. It took 100,000 years at least for the human species to spawn its first billion representatives on the planet. As we enter the new millennium, we are guaranteed to produce a billion every decade and this exponential curve will develop incrementally as the population increases and the time-span decreases. We have now taken over the planet and biological evolution has yielded to cultural evolution. The difference is that the second kind involves the development, not of a variety of species, but of one highly complex species, which does not enjoy manifold forms but is restricted to two: the male and the female. Whatever the truth may be about some recent feminist studies which suggest that there were societies in the past that were matriarchal and/or that valued women in every way that made the female of the species equal to, or more important than the male, three possibilities that concern us presently seem to be significant:

1) The kind of culture that valorises the sign of the sword or the symbol of the blade is essentially male-oriented and patriarchal, emphasising and rewarding the so-called 'masculine virtues' of toughness, aggression and dominance; whereas the cultures that promote the symbol of the chalice or the cup are more inclusive of the feminine dimension, and more inclined towards the so-called 'feminine virtues' of compassion, gentleness and love.

2) Whether the latter kind of culture ever did exist or prevail, it must surely be clear that a balance between these two tendencies should be achieved and maintained even if it has never been so before. The human species is in charge of its own cultural development. It is not like the animal kingdom, prisoner to the laws of its nature, to the instinctive coding in its DNA. We can invent whatever culture we choose to endorse, if we have the collective will to do so. It is a matter of choice.

3) The suggestion that because there are two forms of the one species, male and female, our culture must be either matriarchy or patriarchy, that either the women must dominate the men or vice versa, is simply to transfer the worst features of the culture of the sword onto all culture of every kind. Domination is the hallmark of the patriarchal paradigm. It should be replaced by a paradigm of partnership between the two essential forms which are the female and the male.

Psychologists differ in their views about whether the culture of the sword is endemically masculine, being an extension and external structuralisation of the biology of the male. The physical superiority of the male[10] provides the natural basis for supremacy and domination, although, of course, it does not also supply any kind of justification. 'The human male's political proclivities are… a direct expression of his biological nature… The universal anthropological finding is that politics, like warfare, is an essentially masculine concern…'

Whether this is true, or whether such proclivities are the result of sociological intentionality, cultural bias, psychological priming and/or educational prejudice, the important point is to do something to rectify such a situation. Although it is undeniably true that there are ungainsayable differences between men and women biologically, such differences do not create a discontinuity between the two. Masculinity and femininity are a continuous spectrum on the overarching span upon which men and women tend to be categorised according to development in the direction of either tendency. There are 'effeminite' men, and there are warlike women. Jean Genet and Danny Larue are on the opposite side of the spectrum to Margaret Thatcher and Queen Boadicea. And this spectrum does not exist only in terms of different individual people, it also exists inside the biology and the psychology of each one of us. Each one of us includes an Animus and Anima as an archetypal presence of the male and the female. This was the theory first expounded and named by Jung.

The earliest significant body of evidence we have of how paleolithic man saw the world is the cave paintings of southern Europe from about 15,000 BCE. Artists left the outer entrances and crawled into the darkness to paint these masterpieces on the walls of caves, some more than a kilometre from the entrance.[11]

> The idea of an underground labyrinth, in the depths of which cosmic power is concealed and disclosed, is familiar to us from Greek mythology (notably the Cretan labyrinth of the Minotaur) – an intestinal maze that leads to belly or womb, where life is replenished or extinguished... In the large central sanctuaries of the Magdalenian caves, one finds symbols and paintings of animals in which, according to Leroi-Gourhan,[12] the female principle is being attended by the male. At the cave entrances, in the corridors, and at the furthest 'back-cave' shrines, masculine symbols prevail. He suggests that this may be because the caves themselves are obviously feminine. The overall impression is of a harmonious balance between masculine and feminine... What makes the European caves so thrilling is not just the beauty of the painting but the sense that here, over a period of several thousand years, the paleolithic dream-time was elaborated with a consistency and splendor that qualifies it as one of the world's great religions.

It is interesting to examine the shift that occurred in the Hebrew Bible, for instance, at a time when the canon of the sacred scriptures was being delineated. The so-called 'Priestly' version of the ancestral story was trying to articulate a blueprint for a theocratic state. This purpose had significant influence on the treatment both of women and serpents in the rearranged text.

Christianity certainly became a religion of the sword predominantly after the conversion of the Emperor Constantine. It existed under that banner throughout the fall of the Roman Empire, the so-called Dark Ages and the Middle Ages for the most part, although subtle and unprecedented variations on the theme were played in the time of the troubadours and the chivalric legends of the Holy Grail.

The interesting contrast is with the person and the teachings of Jesus himself. Many writers have based their case for the divinity of Jesus on simple delineation of his unusual personality. Jesus must have been God to have been the kind of man he was. His compassion, vulnerability, non-violent pacificism, openness and gentleness would have been the scorn of any sergeant-major or scout-master training a potential messiah!

In some art and literature the pen is mightier than the sword. Such literature, despite the best efforts of propaganda, despite history being written by the winners, leaves footprints of the marginalised on the edge of the text. This is also what makes it easier to believe in the Gospels as inspired works of art.

We only have to read the stories of our ancestors, the stories of ancient Ireland, ancient Norway, ancient Greece, to understand the unconscious dreamworld that gave birth to the Europe we now inhabit. Examining these myths and legends is a parallel exercise to the examination and appropriation of our own individual world of dreams.

In the fifth century BCE Aeschylus wrote his *Orestia*, a series of three plays: *Agamemnon, The Libation-Bearers* and *The Eumenides*. It was an important time in the history of European thinking. It was the time of the foundation of what we have come to know as Graeco-Roman civilisation, the source of our Western-European culture. These powerfully representative dramas hold an important key to the story of how that civilisation came to be: what it enshrined, what it rejected. In the first of these plays, Agamemnon, king of the Greeks, is about to set sail for Troy to do battle against the kinsmen of Paris who absconded with the fairest woman of the land, Helen, betrothed to Menelaeus, his brother. Agamemnon tricks his wife Clytemnestra into sending their daughter, Iphigenia, to the place where the ships are to set sail, pretending that he intends her to be the bride of Achilles, the greatest warrior of the Greeks. Instead he wants to sacrifice her to the Gods so that the winds may become favourable to Troy. Agamemnon sacrifices his daughter in obedience to the oracle and to fulfil his duty as king and admiral of the fleet.

In the second play he has returned from Troy and is ritually bathing himself to clean away the blood of battle when his wife Clytemnestra captures him in a net and stabs him to death to avenge his murder of Iphigenia.

In the third play of the trilogy, her son Orestes is tried in the temple of Apollo at Delphi for slaying his mother and her new consort Aegisthus, in order to avenge her murder of his father, King Agamemnon. There are twelve jurors, presided over by the goddess Athene. After much agonising and debate, joined by the Chorus of Eumenides who represent the ancient Furies or Fates, upholding the old order of things, as protectors of society and executors of justice, a vote is taken. The score is six votes for each side until Athene casts her vote in favour of Orestes. The decision of the court, voiced by Athene, is that the killing of one's mother is not the shedding of kindred blood. Matricide is not the same as patricide. It is the same argument as Herbert Spencer's in the nineteenth century: women are no more than incubators of male sperm. Society has become irretrievably patrilinear and the chorus of the play is left to lament for Clytemnestra: 'That they should treat me so! I, the mind of the past, to be driven under the ground, outcast, like dirt.' Such dramas identify the shift to a patriarchal structure of society.

Rejection of the feminine, whether as a gender or as a part of oneself, is an essential element in the attempt to divinise ourselves, to make ourselves into angels. It is much easier for a man to imagine that he is disembodied, spiritual, eternal than it is for a woman. He is not as obviously linked to the temporal cycle. He does not have the reality of child-birth, the experience of breast-feeding, the menstrual cycle, to remind him constantly that he is part of a process of generation and decay, one of a family that lives and dies, irretrievably constituted of flesh and blood. It is possible for a man to live in undisturbed fantasy of immortality until ill-health or death shatters his dream. He does not have daily reminders, monthly blood samples, mid-life power-cuts, as unavoidable warning signals and incontovertible evidence of his earthiness, fragility and impermanence. He does not have an inbuilt count-down system which advises him of his flimsiness and warns him of his time limit and sell-by date.

It is understandable that we try to hide the evidence, bury the bodies and throw the alarm-clock down the stairs, which must be part of the motivation to obliterate the 'feminine' both in ourselves and in itself, because it prevents us from being hard, durable and immortal diamonds, embodying, as it does, what is soft, tender, ephemeral. It is also understandable that we try to construct for ourselves a programme of survival and longevity which involves beating the clock, subduing the emotions, conquering the flesh, hardening the body. It is essentially fear of what we are that makes us resent and reject it.

Whatever the explanations, it is true that our culture and so-called 'civilisation' have undervalued and degraded the feminine, both as part of each one of us and as incarnated in over fifty percent of the human race registered as women. And this balance has to be redressed. Whether we do this by creating situations in which women exercise the same authoritarian paradigms as men have done in the past is questionable. It may be necessary as an intermediary shake-up of prevailing structures and institutions. However, it seems to me that the more necessary cultural revolution is one in which we no longer make such stark divisions between the two genders but recognize the continuity of the spectrum in which we all share, in varying degrees, masculine and feminine traits and characteristics.

A specific example of such an overall principle of self-acceptance applies to sexual orientation, where in terms of education, behaviour, identity, dress and demeanour, people have been required, in the past, to be either man or woman. In a culture that also regarded sexuality as primarily geared towards procreation and as prohibited outside marriage, the roles of the two identifiable partners were uncomplicatedly enumerated and their distinctive deportment and behaviour prescribed.

Such facile categorisation must surely give room to reassessment in the light of recent investigation and persistent protest against the inadequacy of such unsophisticated compartmentalisation. Europe, like the giant Polypemon, has to be prevented by some Theseus from trying to squeeze its members into readymade beds by cutting off whatever members fail to fit.

It may have been a necessary strategy for the survival of the human species to insist that all sexual energy be directed towards procreation and the survival of an unlikely species in a lethally hostile world. Annihilation and extinction of the race was a possibility. Now, however, as we enter the twenty-first century, the demographers assure us that we will be adding a further billion people to the family every ten years and that by the end of the next century the number and the timespan will increase and decrease respectively in an incremental and exponential fashion. In such circumstances does it not become obtuse, to say the least, to keep on insisting that all sexual energy must be directed towards people production? Surely any diversification or redirection of this energy must be seen as a welcome decrease in the mounting pressure.

When we hear of the increase in the homosexual population and the decrease both in the desire for and the number of children in the average family in Europe, we should be rejoicing in nature's capacity to adapt and its versatility in face of restricting circumstances, rather than reiterating anachronistic maxims and condemning variations on the stereotyped profiles of men and women, marriages and partnerships.

It must have become abundantly clear by now that all partnership is not with a view to procreation and that all men are not made in the image of Johnny Weissmuller or Sylvester Stallone, nor all women produced in packages modelled on either Maria Goretti or Marilyn Monroe. There is a spectrum of male-female identity and each of us is situated somewhere along that rainbow of possibility that makes our particular sexual identity as personal and as unrepeatable as a finger-print.

# CHAPTER FIVE

# TOP-HEAVY TIN SOLDIERS

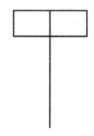

An exaggerated emphasis on the 'spiritual' and a vilification of the 'physical', coupled with an overemphasis on self-contained identity as opposed to being-with-others, colours both our relationship with ourselves and with other people from our earliest years. The culture that presents us with such options also presents us with preferred heroes and saints who are solitary, celibate, rugged, ascetic. Those of us who cannot or will not embrace such ideals or follow such role models are made to feel disappointing or second-rate. It also engenders an ingrained fear of bodily and sexual self-expression.

Such unrealistic and arbitrary cultural ideals, even though they may produce, in exceptional cases, exotic awe-inspiring deeds and personalities, create a schizophrenic tension in most ordinary people. Neglect of and disregard for the emotional and sexual side of ourselves and the other-oriented structure of our bodies and personalities has two inevitable consequences: we develop defence mechanisms and outer armour, which allow us to survive undernourishment of our philanthropic appetites, and we remain undereducated and illiterate in our relational capacity. Those of us who fail to become beautiful anchorites or hermits have to stumble about the market-place feeling insecure, guilty, awkward and angry.

D.W. Winnicott, in his lifelong study of child psychiatry,[13] has shown that, as well as the physical substance that is every child's reality as a body, there is another no less real part of each one of us, which he calls 'potential space'. This relational orbit is neither entirely interior nor entirely exterior. It has to be appropriated and expanded into by each of us, which is not possible unless the child is coaxed into it by a contagious atmosphere of trust. Unless the child can relax and be confirmed by the surrounding environment, it will retire within the confines of the substantial bodily self and the potential space will eventually evaporate. The removal of this dimension not only limits the expansive growth of the child, it also has a detrimental effect on the cauterised remains. The child has to organise its substantial self not in terms of welcoming and out-going transitivity, but in the grip of frightened and hostile defensiveness.

Such a transformation of the body into defensive armour can be partial or total. The face can become a mask from which eyes peep out above a determined chin, preventing any show of emotion. Self-control and stubborn independence make for a stiff-necked race. Chest and shoulders as fortresses make us hard and inaccessible. Reinforced ramparts around the diaphragm cause nervous stomach complaints, even ulcers, and can make pleasurable activity, especially in sexual love, painful or impossible.

It is easy to understand how such armouring of the self might be confused with the virtue of chastity and how victims of internal paralysis can be hailed as paragons of virginity. However, apart from a confused sense of values, the real weakness of such cultivation of the armoured body around the self-contained substance of the self is the incapacity to surrender that it generates. The ethic of no surrender is especially traumatic in face of the two realities that of their nature demand such surrender – love and death. And it is difficult to see how Christianity could have become identified that any such ethic, turning itself into a religion of self-conquest when it was instituted as a religion of self-surrender and when its fundamental axes were the realities of love and death.

In such a context, women's education was separate and geared towards motherhood; the woman's role was presented in terms of 'virgin and martyr' with long-suffering impotence at a personal level being sometimes hailed as sanctity. Virtue is mistaken in such a scenario for an incapacity to accede to any virtue whatsoever. The corresponding ideal of 'manhood' spells harsh and ascetic aggression towards oneself and towards others. For a male to be soft or sentimental is betrayal of the cause. Displays of emotion, whether by tears or gestures, are ridiculed and interpreted as signs of going 'soft in the head'.

In reality, as we have discovered, male and female do not make up any such a clearcut either/or division. Nor is sexuality a stereotyped male versus female enactment to continue and preserve the human race. It is also, and perhaps more importantly, a form of intercommunion, a mutual expression of that instinct for communion which is one of the deepest urges and structural typicalities of our being. The search for shared intimacy and reciprocity is not peripheral or tangential, accidental or ready made. It is a central and essential aspect of who we are, and needs to be taken seriously, treated with reverence and educated with care and expertise.

Education is the transmission of the values and wisdom of any given society. Children are born without culture. Education is the process of enculturation which supplies them with the cultural canopy woven by the particular tribe into which they happen to be born. From earliest times in Western European culture there was a militaristic flavour to education. Sparta, the most flourishing city of the Greeks in the eighth and seventh centuries BCE, brought in an almost exclusively military programme around 550 BCE for education of men who were to become Spartan warriors. The name has remained part of our language to describe such aims and conditions. Everything was organised with a view to military service. Rigorous discipline and austerity hardened up the children whose virility and combativeness were tested and promoted. In the later flowering of Greek educational philosophy, Aristotle, who was tutor to Alexander the Great of Macedonia, shared some of Plato's views about education – that it should be state controlled and for the strict training and formation of citizens. The minority of these would be philosophers, the majority would be useful workers and the major educational effort would be towards training soldiers to protect the state.

The extraordinary fact is that the same pedagogical methods and the same discipline and curriculum were carried on for over a thousand years in Greece and for six or seven centuries in the Roman Empire, which adopted the Greek system with certain adaptations. Christians maintained the educational tradition of the Empire even after it became the Holy Roman Empire. Christians could easily have organised an original system of education on the lines of the Jewish rabbinical schools, where children were taught primarily through the study of the Scriptures, but they preferred to maintain the educational tradition of the Roman Empire even after it had become Christian.

Charlemagne (742-814) has sometimes been represented as the creator of the medieval educational system. However, what he sponsored and promoted can be seen when examined in terms of its sources and its curriculum as a continuation of this same Graeco-Roman inspiration. He did manage to keep scholarship and learning alive in bleak times which enabled the passing of the torch to the later Middle Ages when the blossoming of European education really occurred.

The single greatest influence in all such spheres was Thomas Aquinas in the thirteenth century. His was the definitive and accredited attempt to merge the two traditions of Hellenism and Christianity. The model for his ideally educated person was the 'Scholastic', who was also the model for later clerical culture: one whose rational intelligence dominated and controlled the rest of his human being and whose life was based upon a moral code pursued with belligerent intensity against all the warring impulses and appetites that might threaten the hegemony of sweet reason.

Three tendencies characterised and energised this persistent, homogenous and enduring model of education in European culture: centralisation, rationalism, militarism. Centralisation occurred not just in the mental faculties of the learner but also in the authoritative organisation of the system itself. The most obvious example of this is the system instigated by Napoleon in France at the time when the French were at their most belligerent and militaristic.

In France at the time of the Renaissance, it was the Jesuit schools, with their Jansenistic flavour, which very brilliantly combined the new Humanism, based on the rediscovery of Graeco-Roman culture, with the doctrines of the Roman Catholic Church. However, even though much attention was given to science and the development of human culture, it was not until the French Revolution that the universal right to education was proclaimed in 1791. It was left to Napoleon, however, to implement this ideal. He did it with his own blend of curriculum and control system. The unified state system that he introduced has survived with certain modifications to the present day, and, until our own century, the French system of education was the typical representative of the more generalised European theory.

The establishment of secondary schools for girls was one of the achievements of the Third Republic in 1880. Until the Second World War, however, the curriculum was different from that of the boys' schools. In 1854 France was divided into various educational districts, each one being administered by a rector and each one having a university as the centre of its academic and administative web. The rector was in charge of both the university and of all education within that particular district. Each district was run according to norms and regulations set down and supervised by central government. Thus, the system in France was an exact imitation of the philosophy of centralised rational government, which applied to the human body as much as to the body politic. The Cartesian groundplan, based on the *Cogito ergo sum* ('I think therefore I am') formula, had become the all-prevailing architecture of a totalitarian educational system, with an inexorable and homogenised central authority.

The militaristic tendency is best illustrated in Germany. After the shock of Prussian defeat by Napoleon at the battle of Jena in 1806, a rather nonchalant 'classical' system was radically overhauled. Such reforms reached their zenith in the Nazi educational system from 1933 to 1945. This was no less than an attempt to ensure that totalitarian government had complete control over the whole population. In all places of education it was a question of indoctrinating each child with 'German culture'. An integral part of such induction was the Hitler Youth movement, where a similar programme was implemented along military lines.

Whatever the form or the historical circumstances, it is clear that our philosophies of education, derived mostly from the Graeco-Roman world and sharpened by experiences of war and deprivation, have followed a pattern that has identifiable characteristics. Men and women have been separated from childhood for the purposes of education. The way they were educated was also entirely different. The educational needs and rights of women were not acknowledged or addressed until the late nineteenth century. Education was strictly regulated and put in the hands of a centralised authority with control over the curriculum and intent to brain-wash the population into acceptance of the received culture and philosophy of the country or group who were in charge. For purposes of good goverment and self-defence, the education of the male population had a disciplinary and military bias, which was designed to create a soldierly attitude and a war-like propensity. Whether the war was to be waged on an outside enemy or on oneself for the purpose of self-defence or self-conquest, the virtues to be instilled were the same and the role models were warriors and heroes.

As always, Shakespeare detects the problem, identifies the trend and describes the process and the results in one of his many prophetic dramas. His play *Coriolanus* examines the structures of such an essentially masculine and Roman construct. It presents the point of view that warriors are created by culture and education. No one is the hero of this play. It is not like *Hamlet, Macbeth, Othello, Romeo and Juliet.* Coriolanus is not the name of a hero, it is the name of a town that was conquered by a Roman general. Coriolanus, the man, was called after a conquered and colonised city.

> Ay, Marcius, Caius Marcius! Dost thou think
> I'll grace thee with that robbery, thy stol'n name
> Coriolanus, in Corioles?

The main character in the play is 'a boy of tears' who is victim of an inevitable situation. He is each one of us in military school. He is an anonymous puppet caught in a web of conflicting powers. He is any man or everyman whose life has been taken over by another power, just as Corioli was crushed and colonised by imperial Rome. He has no name, no life, no head, no heart of his own. He is a soldier of the Roman Empire. The other main character in the play is the mob, the crowd. Unlike the first hero without a name, the second hero has many names: it is 'the many-headed hydra': 1st citizen, 2nd citizen, 3rd citizen; 1st senator, 2nd senator; 1st conspirator, 2nd conspirator; 1st guard, etc. The tragedy is played out between the two protagonists. Twenty-five of the twenty-nine scenes of the play involve a crowd of some kind. Twelve of the scenes take place in the market-place, the home of the crowd, the streets or public places of the city; ten take place on the battlefield. In other words the drama unfolds in the public arena where the public servant is manipulated by the faceless body politic he serves. This second character in the play could be described as the Minotaur, if we use that myth to portray the typical features and often devastating effect of the moral majority.

Coriolanus is the child of Roman civilisation. He has been educated for war, he has been trained to do battle, he has had all the tenderness and 'humanity' knocked out of him. So, when peace emerges and he presents himself to the public for election as senator, his military personality works against him in the political arena. He is too haughty to beg for votes, too proud to show his wounds. They hate him and he despises them. So, the mob banish him because they no longer need him. They are no longer under attack so they no longer have to put up with these unbearable pugilistic machines they have created to defend themselves in times of war. He treats their banishment with disdain, calling back to them as he leaves: 'I banish you, there is a world elsewhere.' He then goes to join the enemies of Rome and is used again as a war machine to bring his own city to its knees, which he does without difficulty. So, the city of Rome is to be razed to the ground unless its citizens can persuade the very person they have recently dismissed to relent. They send his wife Virgilia to plead with him and in a poignant moment of silence where she takes him by the hand, he gives in and acquiesces to his own destruction rather than the destruction of Rome. It is a very clever drama in which Shakespeare juxtaposes the political struggle between the aristocrats (the lions) and the wily tribunes of the plebs (the foxes) on the one hand, and the psychological struggle within Caius Marcius himself between the masculine and the feminine (represented by Virgilia, whom he addresses as 'My noble silence, hail!') on the other. She represents that part of Caius Marcius which has never been given any credence or opportunity for self-expression during the time of his concentrated and severe education in the martial arts. These two conflicting forces (the music of Mars, God of War and that of Venus, Goddess of Peace and Love) in his personality correspond to the sociological forces conflicting in the Roman state. Shakespeare is diagnosing the inherent weakness of both Roman civilisation and its educational system. Its tragedy is to have been constructed for warfare and by the same token to have been found impotent to deal with the more sophisticated scenario of peace. Perfect for adolescents in time of war, it was inadequate to cater for an adult population in times of peace. And so to survive it had to create situations that would valorise the heroes which its educational system could not help producing. So situations of war had to be constantly created.

Coriolanus, the town, the man, the tragedy, represent the inevitable crisis of imperialism. Any person, or state, that conquers another, or takes over another, imposing its own personality on that other, is bound to either extinguish that other or run the risk of being extinguished itself.

Volumnia, the mother of Coriolanus, personifies Rome as mother. Her catch-cry is 'Man child must prove himself a man.' Women who are treated as nothing more or less than mothers of men warriors who will glorify the status quo are bound to become culture vultures, vampires for the cause they serve. 'If he had died' she tells her fellow citizens, 'his good report would have been my son.' Volumnia is to her son Coriolanus what Rome is to the Volsces. Her embodiment of motherhood and total identification with this role is destined to breed tragedy. She breeds tragedy from the moment she gives birth to a son. If a mother insists on imposing her will upon her son to the extent that she deprives him of any will of his own, she inevitably destroys him. And if a mother has been born with no other reason for existence than to breed a child who will defend the empire, then she has no option other than to adopt such a role. You either allow your son, your pupil, your colony, your people, to develop fully into their own strange reality or you must destroy them altogether. Anything in between these two possibilities is sure to produce a situation of tragedy: such as we see outside the gates of Rome where a mother is on her knees begging her son to kill himself in order that she may live. With a mother like this, with a government like this, with a culture like this, tragedy is inevitable.

The drama has been played out from Waterloo to Vietnam, from Korea to Kosovo, with countless Coriolanus figures who have been spewed out by our schools, for the most part built on military styles.

And when the Europeans went to the so-called new world, they took this contagion with them. They believed that, because they arrived, the world that was there should begin again. They began to eliminate systematically the 'aliens' who were there before them. This was the colonising mentality in its most basic and brutal form. A film from the 1970s called *Soldier Blue* showed in vividly violent images how American soldiers set about conquering everything or slaughtering everything they encountered as a stranger. The big blue horizons of the new world had to be caged and reduced to a blue uniform. Everything had to conform to our logic or be destroyed, everything had to become uniform, one kind of culture, one kind of existence, or die. Soldiers are the servants of this inexorable law. They blindly obey the order to shoot first and ask questions afterwards. Their lives are regulated by dead principles of service to a code which stitches the very uniform they wear. Conformity to the 'uniform' – one way of being only – protects from any encounter with what is different, other, strange. You wipe out the redskins, the red devils, because they aren't white. You wipe them out in case they might raise their heads and tell you that you don't really exist as a human being until you are prepared to listen to another voice, to move outside the charmed circle of the blue uniform.

The heroine of the film, Candice Bergen, is a white girl who was brought up by the indians, who had captured her as a child. She and one of the Blue soldiers are forced into 'shocking' intimacy, which neither of them would have chosen if circumstances beyond their control had not intervened. This girl is so 'strange' to him. 'I am not an Indian and couldn't live with them', she says 'but I love them enough to know that they must live. This is not our land. And it never will be ours if we destroy everything in it but ourselves.' It is the stranger, the other, the alien, the foreigner, who must eventually show us the true reality of what we are – aliens among strangers, who must open up to the pluralist society that surrounds us, rather than wrap ourselves up in a uniform that identifies us as soldiers who cannot tolerate the existence of anyone who does not belong to the same tribe, who does not wear the same uniform. It is a warlike religion that insists on sacrifice of the alien on the altar of the incumbent.

And the story continues. Another such film, *Patton: Lust for Glory*, also made in the 1970s, shows George C. Scott in an Oscar-winning role as General George S. Patton of the US Army in World War II. Patton is a compulsive war lover as well as a military genius. He acknowledges the sensual kick he gets out of battle, even its aftermath as the maimed and the dead lie around him on the battlefield and the stench is in his nostrils. He was meant to lead the Allied forces as they invaded Europe but one incident ensured the transfer of this responsibility to General Montgomery: In a field hospital in Sicily in 1943, Patton kneels and prays at the bedside of an unconscious soldier whose face is covered in bandages. Then he rises and moves along to another bed where a GI in uniform sits crying. The reason, he explains, is nerves. A victim of combat fatigue, he can face the fighting no longer. Patton's reaction is to bash him on the head, knocking off his helmet, berating him as a coward and even reaching for his pistol before the medical staff intervene.

If such 'men' are in charge, if such psychology is essentially and biologically 'masculine', then it is no wonder that certain women are appalled by the reality that only about twelve percent of those working in the higher echelons of computer technology are women. What kind of monsters are the male psyche likely to produce and what kind of world are they likely to usher in for our children to deal with? Men do not ask themselves questions, some analysts tell us, about the likely results or consequences of their investigations and experiments; they concern themselves simply with what can be achieved, with what combinations can be elucidated, with the furthest horizons of our inventive powers. Such uncontrolled and irresponsible craving for novelty, at the control board of the most advanced technological capacity to create virtually anything we decide to create, should give us pause.

# CHAPTER SIX

# THE FOUR OF THE CROSSROADS
# ✝
# THE SWINGING OF THE DOOR

Geometry is the natural language of the mind. It presents an abstract skeleton of the world around us in a way that is easily digested and understood by the kind of mentality we have. Although it is not the only kind of intelligence we have, it is the one most consistently and rigorously cultivated by prevailing educational systems and establishments.

We have a cultural bias in favour of this scientific way of understanding everything. As long as we understand that bias, there is some hope of redressing the balance in favour of another kind of reality which is impenetrable by such a mentality, and another kind of knowing which can open horizons beyond the world of facts, events and measurable data.

Science sees everything as reducible to a number of universal laws. It then makes interconnections between these. When we see lightning we listen for thunder; when we feel wind we watch for the waves; when we find frost we know why leaves fall. Everything has a reason, an explanation, a cause. Patient observation will inevitably reveal the cause and these causes interconnect to form a set of laws about the world we live in, which offer a satisfactory explanation for all that is. The theoretical ideal of science is to reduce the varied and changing world to a combination of definable elements (chemistry) in terms of their relations to one another as types of energy (physics). All the qualities of difference can be reduced to quantifiable elements. Everything in the world around us and within us can be boiled down to series of material points and elementary movements, which are identifiable and determined with reference to space and time – space being the ordered totality of concrete extensions and time the ordered totality of concrete durations. So, scientific assessment of everything is made in terms of space, time and motion.

These three are standardised in terms of MKS – metres, kilograms and seconds. We have to get an objective viewpoint, which at its most refined would amount to a picture of the world from nobody's point of view. Otherwise subjective elements creep in. We have to provide a language that is unambiguous, each sign or symbol representing an agreed, incontrovertible and exact meaning. Thus a metre was one ten-millionth part of a meridian that passes from the pole to the equator (reproduced in platinum on the official metre stick kept in Paris) until in October 1960 it was universally accepted to be 1,650,753.73 wavelengths of the orange-red light of kyypton 86. The kilogram is unassailably identified as the weight of pure water at its greatest density temperature at sea-level in the volume of 1000 cubic centimetres (called a litre). And finally, the second is incontrovertibly defined as one three-thousandth-six-hundredth of one twenty-fourth part of a period of the earth's rotation on its axis.

All of which means that a world record in the 100 metres sprint can be recorded in any part of the world at any time and, if verified officially, must be accepted as fact by everyone in every other part of the world. The language of scientific formulae is an invariant and universal expression. Other languages are relative. If I say: 'John is here now', my meaning depends on who John is, where I am, and when I happen to be speaking. The sentence could be referring to John the Baptist, John of Gaunt, or Pope John XXIII. The word 'here' could refer to Palestine, England or Italy, and 'now' could relate to the first century BCE, the fourteenth or the twentieth century. In science, no such flexibility, woolliness, or ambiguity is allowed. If there is a cross-roads in Jerusalem, it can be identified, measured, situated exactly. And if there was a cross on Golgotha it should be situated exactly in time, in space and in the causal network of why things happen in the way they do.

But that is not all. Science also understands that such events are dependent upon the testimony of key witnesses – eye-witness accounts, reports from those who were there. Science is aware that most of what we see is illusion. Half the crucifixion for those who were at the foot of the cross was happening outside the visible, audible, understandable spectrum of the key witnesses. Everything we see is made up of the scenery outside our minds and the electro-chemical sensations that this produces in our minds. Basically it is the brain that sees, hears and paints the picture that we flash onto our inner screens and remember. So, science knows that there is nothing happening out there that isn't half painted by whoever is looking at it. Our eyes are curved surfaces with 150 million photoreceptors embedded in the retina. These are sensitive to light, which comes in packages of energy called photons. One photon enters each receptor. The type of radiation that we call light enters the eye and excites the retinal cells causing chemical changes. These cause electrical changes in the optic nerve fibres to which the cells, of the retina are attached. These changes are transmitted in electrical currents along the optic nerve to the visual centre, the picture industry, at the back of the brain. In other words, all information from any one of our senses – smells, noises, tastes, colours, shapes, distances – are transmitted to the central nervous system in the form of electrical currents, which are always the same no matter which particular organ they come through. So, sounds, smells, colours, etc., are fed into the trash compactor that churns them out at the other end as one long homogenous series of electro-magnetic radiation, which is fed to the brain, built to receive and process such data so efficiently and so immediately that folks at the turnstiles don't even know there is a translation process going on. They think, and we think, that light, heat, sound, etc., are completely different things because they go in one ear or attack one finger. However, contemporary theories of radiation make us see all these phenomena as different notes on the same piano, or separate strips on one large extended electro-magnetic field. Every sensation that hits any one of our taste-buds, our nostrils, our eyes or our ears, is one kind of electro-magnetic wave, which differs from the others only in its magnitude and its period. Science measures these wavelengths.

What we call the visible spectrum is a very limited area, a tiny segment of reality, which we are able to see. If we stick to our image of the piano and talk about it musically, sight would represent only one single octave on the total scale. Within this very limited, short-sighted perspective we see what we imagine to be all the colours of the rainbow but, in fact, we are nearly as blind as bats in comparison with what could be seen if this area of the radiation process was less restricted. If we move 30 octaves beyond the red side of the rainbow spectrum, as opposed to the violet, we would come to the sphere of radio waves, the sound studio, which is 30 doors down on the same corridor, past what we call the infra-red rays, these being beyond the scope of our red register. And on the other side beyond the ultra-violet rays, about 8 to 16 octaves higher, we pass the Hertz waves studios and carry on until we hit X-rays and gamma rays.

Science deals with everything on this corridor of sensation in the same way. Laws of reflection, refraction, interference, emission, polarisation, absorption, etc., which apply to light can also be applied to heat rays. In other words, the totality of radiation processes can be represented by science in a strictly unitary form, according to a definite 'index' which designates the wavelength of the different kind of ray and distinguishes these by their numerical and positional value. The nature of a body hanging on a cross, for instance, is not determined by its physical or sensory manifestation, but by its atomic weight, its specific heat, its exponents of refraction, its index of absorption, its electrical conductivity, its magnetic susceptibility. This is the universal and invariant language of science. The theory of relativity is an attempt to achieve a conception of the world from the view-point of no one in particular, according to Eddington. The dream of science is to explain the universe in a single equation, to elaborate its meaning in a series of irrefutable and undeniable propositions.

The double danger about this is that we think it is an advance and we think it is an improvement. In fact it is neither. It is just another way of thinking, which has its own merits and limitations. We have been taught to believe that we have moved from a mythological way of thinking to an enlightened or scientific way of thinking and that this has parallelled the evolutionary process from the stone age to the global village. It isn't true. There are at least two ways of thinking, one is mythological and the other is scientific and it depends upon what you are thinking about as to which one will serve you better under the circumstances. When dealing with the intervention of the divine in human history, scientific analysis is as useful as a sieve would be for grasping liquids. The mythological intelligence is more suited to such unnatural, metaphysical (meaning among other things, beyond physics) visitations. That is why most religious experience has been elucidated in mythological language. The obsession in our century to reduce all understanding to one particular process led to the 'demythologisation' of the scriptures and other testimonies of extraterrestrial interventions in our world. Such a process leaves us with the empty crater, the hole through which the bullet passed, the empty tomb, as the object of our study. It is almost like painting a picture of an aeroplane gone out of sight. Demythologisation in such circumstances leaves us with a handful of dust.

Myth is not something we grow out of. It doesn't develop into science. It is another way of understanding, of approaching, of coping with experiences and happenings which are beyond the competence and the scope of science. This is not to belittle science or to deny its prowess and spectacular achievements, especially in the last three centuries; it is simply to reaffirm that there is more in heaven and earth than such philosophy ever dreamed of. And part of that dream is the very strange involvement of God with humankind. The God who reveals this love remains a hidden God. Revelation never becomes a body of truths that any institution can pride itself on possessing.

The sign of the cross need not be embodied or enveloped in a philosophy or an idea at all. The space of the cross is never geometrical space, where every point and length and breadth and depth is homogenous, invariant and calculable. Mythical thinking, like sensation itself, is always variable and every point, element, and direction in it has a taste, a timbre and a tonality of its own. Both physiological and mythical space differ from metric space: right, left, behind, above, below are not interchangeable. Unlike Euclidean geometry, which posits on all sides of every place homogeneity of position and direction, so that a cross must be a point around which the globe of 360 degrees must circle, with an arm of 90 degrees and a transom beam of 180 degrees, the cross of reality and of the mythic imagination can never be a fixed term in a universal relation which can recur identically. It is a symbol and as such is 'a vortex or cluster of fused ideas' which is endowed with energy, to borrow Ezra Pound's description of another kind of image. The cross is a universal symbol which is shared by every culture, it embraces every interpretation and is open to all angles of vision. It speaks to any person in any place at any time in a direct and personal way. It also carries and incorporates values, ideals and world-views projected onto it by empires and nations who have rallied to it as a banner and used it for their own purposes. To pin it down to any one particular design is an impoverishment. There are so many possible designs based on this motif.

And there is no doubt that the 'sign of the cross' was paramount for early Christianity. It was as important to it as circumcision was to the Jews. For Saint Paul it was 'the hidden wisdom of God' made manifest. Knowledge of this mystery was a secret wisdom, the true 'gnosis' (II Cor. 4:6) of which Paul was the steward. He uses gnostic terminology to describe this mystery of Christ. The mystery is the secret as opposed to the 'kerygma' which is the proclaimed message, which is always a derived and secondary form of the original inexpressible reality. The mystery (*mysterion*) is the eternal counsel (wisdom/sophia) of God before the world began (I Cor. 2:7), hidden in God (Eph 3:9) and made manifest by the cross of Christ which is a 'scandal' and a 'stumbling block' to those who do not believe but which is actually 'indwelling in believers' (Col 1:27) who are initiates. Paul himself, as steward of the mystery, is also a prophet because he is acquainted with the mysteries. The special gift of the prophet (1 Cor. 13:2) is to 'penetrate the mysteries of God'. But this mystery remains silent, it is not expressible in terms other than itself. It is venerated as a sign and is the focus of cultic ritual ceremony but can never be translated into propositions or formulae. The crucial text is I Corinthians 1:17-18 where Paul makes it clear that he was not sent to preach the cross in terms of philosophy, in which it cannot be expressed, because 'the language of the cross is illogical'. For the Jews it is an 'obstacle they cannot get over'; for the pagans it is 'madness'. And Paul says he came to us not with any 'show of oratory or philosophy', rather the only knowledge he claimed to have 'was about Jesus, and only about him as the crucified Christ'.

The cross of Christ as the central emblem of the wisdom and power of God, the original sign of the new life that had erupted on earth, remained an arcane secret tradition, incapable of being translated into available terminology. It was passed on as one of the traditions received from the apostles in unwritten form and subject to the discipline of silence and secrecy. It was a hidden source of unwritten customs and mysteries (sacramental and liturgical life) of the Church, which was prior to and necessary for an understanding of Scripture, as the written expression of the same mystery. All of which points to the 'mysterical' character of Christian knowledge, which always remains a gnostic wisdom, as eloquently expressed in art works and crucifixes as it is in sacred scripture. Liturgy has always been primary theology for Christianity. Credal formulae, for instance, which received such attention and preferment in later periods, have always remained a secondary form of theology.

However, the secret, cultic mystery of the cross inevitably entered the history of the world as a logo, a bill-board, a banner, a poster, a proclamation, an encyclical, a manifesto. There is a politics of the cross as well as a poetry of the cross.

Tertullian (ca. 200) shows its almost obsessional usage from the earliest periods of Christianity: 'at every step forward, at every going in and out, when we put on our clothes and shoes ... in all ordinary customs of everyday life, we trace the sign.'

Presumably, however, its warlike connotations date from the Emperor Constantine, who, a century later, saw a vision of a cross before the battle of the Milvian bridge and was told that he would conquer under this sign. He made Christianity the official religion of his Empire and changed its capital city to Byzantium, which he called Constantinople, after himself. His mother, St Helena, according to later tradition, discovered the remains of the original cross of the crucifixion in Jerusalem. Whatever the truth in these rumours, the emphasis for the next centuries was on militant Christianity, and where it was not sponsoring actual military conquests, it was a symbol of Christ's victory over the devil, and of Christian warfare against evil, sin, and the temptations of the flesh. It became the mighty tree which 'the young warrior' God himself climbed in *The Dream of the Rood,* and the victorious standard or military ensign of the sixth-century hymns of Venantius Fortunatus, *Vexilla Regis* and *Pange Lingua,* which have been sung every year since they were composed in the Roman Catholic Church's celebration of the Passion.

In 1095 Pope Urban II launched the crusades in a rabble-rousing speech which put Christendom at war with the Muslims for the next two centuries. The word 'crusade' comes from the Latin and French words for cross, and everyone who went to war in this cause was entitled to wear a cross on their battle-dress.

In seventeenth-century Germany the Rosicrucian movement was

founded, its emblem being the combination of a rose and a cross. It was supposed to have derived from Christian Rosenkreuz (1484), but later speculation suggests that he was a pious invention. This movement was an attempt to restore the more mystical and mysterious dimensions of the cross and was the source of many esoteric religious movements in the next three centuries in Europe.

The culmination of European warlike appropriation of the symbol of the cross was Nazi Germany's adoption of the swastika as its national emblem. This equilateral cross with arms bent at right angles in the same rotary direction, usually clock-wise, has been a universal symbol for religions from the Buddhists and the Hindus to the Celts and the North American Indians. The word comes from the Sanskrit 'svastika' which means 'conducive to well-being'. In the Hindu usage the right hand bend at the end of the arms was a solar symbol, representing the sun or the light, whereas the left-hand bend or anti-clockwise swastika represented the dark or the night-time realm of the goddess Kali. So, the German swastika would signify an over-emphasis on light and a neglect, once again, of the dark.

The poetry of the cross reached back into the Jewish prophets for whom the tree of life in the Garden of Paradise, watered by the four rivers (Gen. 2:9-10), was the symbol of God's salvation and the wisdom of God. It was the tree of knowledge. The author of the New Testament Apocalypse promises to feed those who are victorious 'from the tree of life set in God's paradise'(2:7). Between these two trees, the early Christians saw the tree of the cross as the same tree of life on which our fate as human beings was decided. In medieval art, Adam's skull was represented at the foot of the cross, because they knew that the cross was erected where Adam was buried. Round it flow the four rivers of paradise. On his deathbed, the legend went, Adam sent his son Seth to paradise to bring him the fruit of immortality from the tree of life. The angel gave him three seeds from which grew a threefold tree out of the dead Adam's mouth, made of cedar, pine and cypress. This is the tree that the soldiers cut down to make the cross of Christ.[14] Such elaborate stories are part of the rich understanding and veneration of the cross in early Christianity. Such mythological elaboration is a profound expression of the depth and the abundance of the understanding of this mystery as something so unique and so generous that it breaks through all attempts to classify it.

The third century Pseudo Chrysostom writes: 'Immortal tree, it extends from heaven to earth. It is the fixed pivot of the universe, the fulcrum of all things, the foundation of the world, the cardinal point of the cosmos. It binds together all the multiplicity of human nature. It is held together by invisible nails of the spirit in order to retain its bond with the Godhead. It touches the highest summits of heaven and with its feet holds fast the earth, and it encompasses the vast middle atmosphere in between with its immeasurable arms.'

Such panegyrics were accompanied by the most elaborate representations of the cross in every kind of precious metal and ornamentation, which eventually offended the sensibilities of the more ascetic and astringent Christians.

In his poem 'The Cross', John Donne (1572-1631) tried to counteract Protestant revulsion to the image of the cross and the attempt of the Reformers to replace the cross in English churches with the Royal Arms. He sees the cross in every aspect of nature including each one of ourselves standing erect with arms outstretched:

> Who can deny me power, and liberty
> To stretch mine arms, and mine own cross to be?
> Swim, and at every stroke, thou art thy cross,
> The mast and yard make one, where seas do toss.
> Look down, thou spiest out crosses in small things;
> Look up, thou seest birds raised on crossed wings;
> All the globe's frame, and sphere's, is nothing else
> But the meridians crossing parallels.

The spirituality of the Middle Ages and the more morose nineteenth-century spirituality emphasised the Man of Sorrows, the

Suffering Saviour, and the cross became a crucifix, with sometimes the most gory representations of the dying body of Christ. This aspect of the total mystery overshadowed all the rest and people were encouraged to revel in their own suffering and afflictions, of whatever kind, in solidarity and sympathy with the suffering servant.

For many years now it has been the tradition in the Philippines to re-enact the crucifixion on Good Friday. Penitents are scourged with glass-studded whips, and thousands of spectators watch under a hot sun as men are nailed and hoisted on fifteen-foot crosses fifty miles north of Manila. The Filipino 'Christs', accompanied by horse-riding men dressed as Roman centurions, parade for at least a mile from the village chapel to the mound, surrounded by barbed wire, in the middle of a rice paddy amid chants of 'Crucify them, Crucify them.'

The projection of our own pathology and the geometries of distortion are legion. Fixation upon any one particular aspect of the total mystery is missing the point, is swapping the glory for the gore, trading our birthright for a mess of pottage. The crucifixion is not a fact. It cannot be nailed down to one explanation, labelled with one easy heading. It is an event. It incorporates the whole drama of God's love for us and our new existence in Him. To concentrate upon the cross as an instrument of torture and death is to wrap ourselves in the cocoon when we should be in flight with the butterfly. Rainer Maria Rilke makes an interesting observation:

> I cannot conceive that the *cross* should *remain*, which was, after all, only a cross-roads. It certainly should not be stamped on us on all occasions like a brand-mark. For is the situation not *this*: he intended simply to provide the loftier tree, on which we could ripen better. He, on the cross, is this new tree in God, and we were to be warm, happy fruit, at the top of it.
>
> We should not always talk of what was *formerly*, but the *afterwards* should have begun. This tree, it seems to me, should have become so one with us, or we with it, and *by* it, that we should not need to occupy ourselves continually with

it, but simply and quietly with God, for his aim was to lift us up into God more purely... Instead of setting out from the place of the crossroads where this sign was high and lifted up into the night of his sacrifice, instead of proceeding onwards from this place of the cross, Christianity has settled down there and claims that it is living there in Christ.[15]

# CHAPTER SEVEN

# THE LABYRINTH

The considerations presented in the first part of this book might seem very far removed from the everyday lives of ordinary people. However, they make up the fundamental options upon which societies are structured and they need to be unearthed and examined if we are to have any comprehensive understanding of our situation.

Such basic presuppositions underpin our upbringing and education, which, in turn, train us to accept without question or even consciousness these basic assumptions on which the structures of our lives are built. A vicious circle naturally ensues, which eventually develops into a labyrinth. This replaces the instinctual programme encoded into the life-patterns of all the other creatures on the earth. It is an artificial limb grafted onto what was originally intended as a free-floating, unencumbered body, which could meet up with and adjust itself to the environment it found itself in.

Quick-thinking adaptability connected with malleable plasticity was the ingenious characteristic that allowed the human organism to survive under the most inimical circumstances. However, such versatile mutability, the posture of a chameleon, is so insecure, unstable and demanding, that the bulk and natural tendency of our embodied reality takes over and imposes itself. We want to be automatons, we prefer to have our schedule organised, we don't want to be overwhelmed by possibility. The forces of nature want to grow a roof over our heads where none was intended. We are naturally inclined to build elaborate nests, immovable dams, honeycombed hives and subterranean anthills. Our automatic response to complexity and danger is to construct an indestructible labyrinth around the Minotaur of our deepest, most vulnerable and breakable selves. We are all aware of this force of gravity in ourselves, the compelling drive towards universal compendiums and general explanations of the world, to borrow phrases from Karl Marx. We long for the harmonious luxury of certitude expressed in 'the geometrical absolutism of an orthodoxy.'

But the truth of our condition is that such luxuries are debilitating and destructive illusions. Just when we are at our most secure and self-satisfied, the unexpected change occurs and we succumb. We have to keep moving, keeping up with what is happening around us. No inhabitant of this planet can stay put or remain static.

In a book called *Hidden Histories of Science*, five of the most gifted scientific writers in the world tell us in a series of essays how science is influenced by culture and how misleading images and entrenched prejudices have distorted our view of life. The notion of evolution, for instance, or development, even etymologically, is mistakenly assumed to be the revelation of an already immanent structure or the unfolding of an already encoded and implicit pre-existing history. These scientists suggest that such a model is inadequate and fails to do justice to the complexity of survival strategies and the creative ingenuity required of us to initiate and maintain the kind of life that establishes the delicate balance between sovereignty and surrender.

It is not enough to obey laws that are already laid down; we have to create patterns and structures which are life-enhancing and which have never existed before. 'Every species is in the process of creating and re-creating, both beneficially and detrimentally, its own conditions of existence, its own environment.'[16] And we, as human beings, have a particularly vigilant and versatile role to play, being the quick-change artists of the planet. Some neurologists even suggest that, far from being genetically determined or assigned to fixed nuclei or modules in the brain, our higher cortex, where our higher learning occurs, is a malleable surface, 'uncommitted at birth', whose development 'depends on the particularities of life experience.' In other words, these scientists are sympathetic to the notion that our nature, far from being a static, pre-existing, unchangeable program, is, at the higher levels of its development, 'an emerging, self-creating whole,' which not only adapts to its environment but 'emerges under the influence of experience.'[17]

This would mean that there could be no possibility of someone in the sixth century BCE, or the first or the thirteenth century CE, legislating for appropriate human behaviour in absolute terms. We are changing, we are the creative architects of our own evolution. This does not mean that we embrace the pragmatic and entirely opportunistic strategy of a situation ethics. It does mean that we reject the eternal, ever-present, pre-determined and pre-determining structure, substance and texture of a so-called natural law that would imply that we who live in the twentieth century and are about to enter the twenty-first century are irrevocably and irredeemably the same as those members of our species who have inhabited the planet since time began.

We are different because we have made ourselves different. This difference has been a combination of environment and the human organism in a co-operative mutation. Those who have been most effective and inspirational in both detecting the changes necessary and imagining the adaptations to be accomplished have been artists and geniuses of one kind or another.

At an individual level, art can be, not just a protest against loss of identity or integrity in the movement of the mob, the programme for the people, the vision statement for the group, the architecture of the sheep-fold or the corralling of the herd, it can also be, more positively, an expression of individuality, of irreducible uniqueness, of idiosyncratic personal quirkiness, which may seem unusual, bizarre, outrageous, obscene, even lunatic at the time of articulation, and may cause public uproar and official condemnation within the labyrinth, but which later reveals itself to represent not just genuine and valid expression of human being and behaviour, in the case of one individual person, but excavation of a reality that lies in the undercrust of the life of each one of us.

There are so many examples of this: D.H. Lawrence's *Lady Chatterley's Lover*, Joyce's *Ulysses*, Hardy's *Jude the Obscure*. Hardy's novels were so excoriated by the public of his time that he turned to poetry instead, which held the truth more succinctly and poignantly, but which fewer people could encounter or understand.

Joyce claimed that *Ulysses*, recently declared to be both the most important and the most read novel in the English language, contained simply the ordinary thoughts of an ordinary man during an ordinary day of the year during his very ordinary life. When the case against Joyce was taken by the censorship board of America, who sought to defend their citizens from such pornography, the lawyer speaking on behalf of America the pure claimed that, in the course of one of the ordinary days of his most ordinary life, he never had even one of the ordinary thoughts that are hideously portrayed in this book. To which the lawyer defending Joyce replied: 'Well sir, you do not have the privilege of being a Celt in the season of Spring.' This somewhat racist remark suggests that each particular culture has the particular task of articulating the precise texture and flavour of its own specific blend of humanity.

If it is true that a labyrinth, constructed out of the false geometries already delineated, once extended throughout the Western world, that this was the course our cultural history took, why concentrate such attention on Ireland as if it were the only perpetrator of such a crime against humanity? How and why should we be responsible for a labyrinth created in ancient Greece?

The answer is twofold. On the one hand, the circumstances of Irish geography and history allowed us to achieve a perfection of this paradigm rarely attained in other less compact and homogenous parts of the world. On the other hand, because we have come to identify these options with the deepest and dearest principles of our religious, social and ethical creeds, it is possible that we might continue to preserve our own particular labyrinth with all the fervour of a threatened minority, imagining ourselves to be the last bastion of purity, when the rest of Western civilisation has begun to understand and escape from such limiting and deforming structures.

One of the many factors specific to our situation, which has contributed to the formation of our particular design of labyrinth, is what has been called in French *le Catholicisme du type Irlandais.*

From the very beginning of our history as a newly formed independent twentieth-century state, our labyrinth was almost conciously designed and implemented. Both the Church and the government were obsessed with warding off the constant threat to Catholic purity from foreign, most especially English, influences. This was most explicit in the hectoring sermons and blatant propaganda of *The Catholic Bulletin* and *The Catholic Mind,* which were set up for the purpose of supervising the rigorous enforcement of Catholic morality.

But at an even less detectable level, magazines dating from the 1920s, such as *Our Boys,* were launched for the specific purpose of conducting the 'Angelic Warfare for Maintaining the National Virtue of our Country.' This particular campaign was based upon twin ideologies of the time. The first was the belief in the racial superiority of the Irish in terms of sexual morality. The second was the puritanical views on sex of the Catholic clergy. The aim of the campaign was to shield the young from 'bad' books and films. It won a major victory in the Censorship of Publications Act of 1929.

Moral policing was required and imposed by the Catholic hierarchy, who were worried about the multiplication of occasions of sin in many new-fangled entertainments, especially the dance-halls. 'Company keeping under the stars of night had succeeded in too many places to the good old Irish custom of visiting, chatting and story-telling from one house to another, with the rosary to bring all home in due time', was the view of one archbishop in 1926. In 1927 the bishops issued a joint pastoral: 'The evil one is forever setting his snares for unwary feet. At the moment, his traps for the innocent are chiefly the dance-hall, the bad book, the indecent paper, the motion picture, the immodest fashion in female dress – all of which tend to destroy the characteristic virtues of our race.' Once again the twentieth century in all its technological manifestations and cultural fashions is pitted against an almost racist view of Irish purity.

This decrying of moral laxity was not just an Irish phenomenon. All over Europe after the Great War there was a fear of degenerate moral behaviour. But, in Ireland, the new Republic was particularly singleminded and fanatical about establishing its own national dugout. This battle for the citadel became polarised into two camps, those defending a Gaelic nationalism and those promoting a cosmopolitan internationalism. Since most of the intelligentsia were protestant, it turned into a war between cultures, those who were in the Gaelic-Catholic mould and those who sought for a pluralist international outlook. Spokespersons from each side – Catholic politicians who publicly vaunted the fact that they were not intellectuals, on the one hand, and Protestant intellectuals like AE and Shaw, on the other – presented almost contrary views on the architecture of the new nation-state. Shaw called for the abandonment of nationalism, saying that it must be added 'to the refuse pile of superstitions' and pointing out that anyone who wanted to divide the race into 'elect Irishmen' and 'reprobate foreign devils (especially Englishmen) had better go and live on the Blaskets where he can admire himself without much disturbance.' The Irish language was going to be a way of cutting off influences from outside. AE was afraid it was being used as 'a dyke behind which every kind of parochialism could shelter.' He wanted 'world culture, world ideas, world science; otherwise Ireland would not be a nation but a parish.' He used *The Irish Statesman*, founded in 1923, as the vehicle for his ideas. 'The cultural implications of the words *Sinn Fein* are evil', he wrote in 1925, 'We are not enough for ourselves. No race is. All learn from each other. All give to each other. We must not be afraid of world thought or world science. They will give vitality to our own nationality. If we shut the door against their entrance we shall perish intellectually, just as if we shut the door against the Gaelic we shall perish nationally.'

Whatever the causes, the doors were shut, culturally, and we remained imprisoned in our own cultural labyrinth. Critics of AE were perhaps justified in questioning his naivety. How would he hope, in the words of one critic, 'to resist the tremendous, vulgarising power of Anglo-American civilisation.' Anyway, the battle for cosmopolitanism was lost. In the words of one recent historian 'There was a naive popular belief that, left alone, Ireland would be a paradise.'[18] The hierarchy seemed to believe that Irish dancing was exempted from the disgrace that hovered over the foreign variety. 'Irish dances do not make degenerates' according to *The Irish Catholic Directory* for 1926.

Another explanation for why the whole population of Ireland was so biddable and ready to be herded into the lonely labyrinth in the first half of this century is offered by historian F. S. L. Lyons. As the population had been halved in the second part of the nineteenth century by the Famine and emigration, the attitude towards the land was deeply affected. The evil to be avoided was subdivision of the farm. The normal procedure was to pass on the farm to the eldest son. 'This meant not only that the favoured son had to delay marriage until the death of both his parents allowed him to enter into his inheritance, but that the other sons, and often enough the daughters as well, were condemned either to emigration or to chastity.'[19] He points out that premarital virginity was not just a moral requirement for a girl but a social one. 'To destroy a girl's "character" by intercourse outside wedlock was regarded in peasant eyes as "murder" and actually so called in some parts of the country.'

Sport was viewed as a vital means of building character and expressing national identity. There were proposals to stage an Irish Olympic Games as early as 1922. The Gaelic Athletic Association (GAA) became the most successful sporting and cultural organisation in the country. Until 1971 this organisation not only banned its members from playing 'foreign' games but even from attending them. It also remained a thirty-two county organisation despite political partition.

The labyrinth in the title of this chapter represents the complex structure of socio-political, religious, educational and psychological ideologies which we enter at birth as our cultural heritage and from which there is no easy escape. Culture is universal. Every one of us comes wrapped inside it. It is also particular and local. It is different for every part of the planet and at every time a child is born. So there can be no definitive antidote. Each manifestation of it requires the particular genius of the particular place to provide its own pioneering trail-blazers who can lead the people out of bondage. Each tribe has to give birth to its own Theseus to find its way out of the labyrinth that, of necessity, constitutes its cultural strait-jacket.

'It is sufficient for one person to think', Edmund Husserl is reported to have said, 'for a whole generation to be saved.' But 'thinking' in this context has to be more than the logical workings of the culturally situated mind. It has to be the work of imagination. The work of a certain kind of artist capable of imagining a brave new world quite different from the one into which such a faculty was born. Such imaginative work can only be done locally, even though its results can become universally proclaimed and paradigmatic for other explorers.

Theseus slew the Minotaur and escaped from the labyrinth by taking two precautions: he forced Daedalus, the architect of the labyrinth, to reveal its shape and contours, and he tied to the doorway the ball of silken thread, given to him by Ariadne, which he unwound as he made his way, thus leaving him a guideline to chart his way out.

# CHAPTER EIGHT

# THE SILKEN THREAD

'If a way to the better there be', Thomas Hardy suggests, 'it exacts a full look at the worst.' He was one of the artists at the end of the last century and the beginning of this one who saw the inhumanity that industrialisation was likely to bring to England. His poem 'The Darkling Thrush' was written on the last day of the nineteenth century, as the century we have just been through was about to begin:

> I leant upon a coppice gate
> When Frost was spectre-gray,
> And Winter's dregs made desolate
> The weakening eye of day.
> The tangled bine-stems scored the sky
> Like strings of broken lyres,
> And all mankind that haunted nigh
> Had sought their household fires.
>
> The land's sharp features seemed to be
> The Century's corpse outleant,
> His crypt the cloudy canopy,
> The wind his death-lament.
> The ancient pulse of germ and birth
> Was shrunken hard and dry,

And every spirit upon earth
Seemed fervourless as I

At once a voice arose among
The bleak twigs overhead
In full-hearted evensong
Of joy illimited;
An aged thrush, frail, gaunt, and small,
In blast-beruffled plume,
Had chosen thus to fling his soul
Upon the growing gloom.

So little cause for carolings
Of such ecstatic sound
Was written on terrestrial things
Afar or nigh around,
That I could think there trembled through
His happy good-night air
Some blessed Hope, whereof he knew
And I was unaware.

It paints a gloomy picture. The last day of 1899 was like a death-lament for the century's corpse. And yet in the midst of this 'growing gloom' a still small voice is heard. It is a thrush, who represents the sound of 'some blessed Hope' of which the rest of the landscape and the rest of humankind is unaware. This is the voice of the artist.

Hardy wrote the following poem in 1914, the year when the First World War began. It is about the sinking of the *Titanic* on the night of 14 April 1912. It is interesting how this event seems to have mesmerised our entire century. Art, if we are prepared to give the cinema such a name, seems to have ended the century with the same striking image: some 2 billion people, the largest audience ever to have witnessed any event in the past, have gone to see the film *Titanic*, which captured the imagination of the whole world.

## The Convergence of the Twain
*Lines on the loss of the 'Titanic'*

I
In a solitude of the sea
Deep from human vanity,
And the Pride of Life that planned her, stilly couches she.

II
Steel chambers, late the pyres
Of her salamandrine fires,
Cold currents thrid, and turn to rhythmic tidal lyres.

III
Over the mirrors meant
To glass the opulent
The sea-worm crawls – grotesque, slimed, dumb, indifferent.

IV
Jewels in joy designed
To ravish the sensuous mind
Lie lightless, all their sparkles bleared and black and blind.

V
Dim moon-eyed fishes near
Gaze at the gilded gear
And query: 'What does this vaingloriousness down here?' …

VI
Well: while was fashioning
This creature of cleaving wing,
The Immanent Will that stirs and urges everything

VII
Prepared a sinister mate
For her – so gaily great –
A shape of Ice, for the time far and dissociate.

VIII
And as the smart ship grew
In stature, grace, and hue,
In shadowy silent distance grew the Iceberg too.

IX
Alien they seemed to be:
No mortal eye could see
The intimate welding of their later history,

X
Or sign that they were bent
By paths coincident
On being anon twin halves of one august event,

XI
Till the Spinner of the Years
Said 'Now!' And each one hears,
And consummation comes, and jars two hemispheres.

Hardy's poem has many possible interpretations. At the beginning of the century, for him, the loss of the *Titanic* symbolised the clash between the old world of nature and the new world of science and industrialisation. Many of his novels treat of the destruction of rural England and manual methods of farming, with the introduction of machinery and industrial technology. The *Titanic* represented the triumph of science and human technology over the destructive forces of nature in terms of the sea. This ship was unsinkable according to its Belfast makers. But such machines also introduced a kind of carnage and destruction, whether through organised warfare or haphazard accident, never before suffered or witnessed by the human species. The Victorians had a morbid fascination with train crashes and shipwrecks, which became the subject of so many paintings and poems.

As we come to the end of the twentieth century, another interpretation becomes possible. The ship represents successful and glamorous progress along the surface of the ocean. The iceberg represents that part of ourselves, our lives, which lies buried beneath our consciousness. The discovery of the 'night-world' of the unconscious at about the same time as Hardy was writing this poem, revealed that human beings were far more complex and extensive than science and medicine had supposed up to that time. The iceberg has often been used as an image of the unconscious, that vast continent beneath the ordinary everyday surface of our lives, to which we gain access through our dreams and which we ignore at our peril, because: 'as the smart ship grew/ In stature, grace, and hue,/ In shadowy silent distance grew the Iceberg too.'

Art is also a way of gaining access to this underworld. The novel, at its most subtle, is able to give utterance to such depths in ourselves, which we hardly recognize until we see it before our eyes in writing. But once we see it and read it we recognize that this was something lurking at the back of our minds which we were never able to identify or articulate for ourselves. Sometimes, indeed, we were quite unaware of it at all until the novel jolted us into recognition of its presence. D. H. Lawrence formulates this in an essay called 'Why the Novel Matters'. His claim is that the well-written novel is like a cardiograph of a life that is lived. So many of us are dead people walking. Some of us don't begin to live until lunchtime. Others are under an anaesthetic while they are at work and they 'live for' the week-ends. I remember a boy at boarding school writing an essay in which he maintained that the only time he was really alive was on the train journey from the school to his home at holiday time. All time at school was something to be put down. He found himself 'killing time' until the end of term. The excitement of release was life at its most lively. Once he hit the platform at the other end, there they all were, his parents and family, as tedious as ever and the jellied monotony of family life congealed around him. The novel can both sensitize you to the deadness of your own existence, the falseness of so-called entertainment, the compliant servitude of most domestic and workaday routine, the inauthenticity of most networks of social relationships. Because 'in the novel you can see, plainly, when the man goes dead, the woman goes inert. You can develop an instinct for life, if you will, instead of a theory of right and wrong, good and bad.' This is what you cannot learn from other sources. Again according to Lawrence: 'The philosopher because he can think, decides that nothing but thoughts matters ... As for the scientist, he has absolutely no use for me so long as I am man alive. To the scientist, I am dead. He puts under the microscope a bit of dead me, and calls it me ... Now I absolutely flatly deny that I am a soul, or a body, or a mind, or an intelligence, or a brain, or a nervous system, or a bunch of glands, or any of the rest of these bits of me. The whole is greater than the part ... For this reason I am a novelist. And being a novelist, I consider myself superior to the saint, the scientist, the philosopher and the poet, who are all great masters of the different bits of man alive, but never get the whole hog. The novel ... can make the whole man alive tremble.' Like the Jewish Rabbi who said that the Bible was not so much a theology about God for humankind, but an attempt to explain humankind to God, Lawrence continues, 'In this sense, the Bible is a great confused novel. You may say it is about God. But it is really about man alive. Adam, Eve, Sarah, Abraham, Isaac, Jacob, Samuel, David, Bathsheba, Ruth, Esther, Solomon, Job, Isaiah, Jesus, Mark, Judas, Paul, Peter: what is it but man alive from start to finish? Man alive, not mere bits.'

It was something of a similar conviction that made Iris Murdoch write novels also. She was a trained philosopher and taught at Oxford all her working life. Yet she felt that the categories of philosophy were a weave of net too large to capture the essential individuality and irreplaceable uniqueness of the human person in lived concrete circumstances. Her first novel was called *Under the Net*. It went below that carefully embroidered network of categories supposed to apply to everyone scientifically and logically. And once it got under that net it could begin to weave the strange unpredictable course of quirky, idiosyncratic private lives.

So, the novel can provide as accurately and subtly as possible our side of the religious equation: what it feels like to be a human being. This can be done to protest against oppressive conditions that prevent the full flowering of this reality, or it can be done to provide a paradigm that will help us to understand and fully develop that particular blend of human genius which is peculiar to each individual.

In other words, art as defender of the orthodoxy of humanity can take on either an individual or a collective voice. It can be a protest against the way in which a whole group, a whole country, a whole culture is leading its people. It can try to show us that as a Western European Culture, as an Irish nation, or even as a particular community, we have been journeying on the *Titanic* for a whole century, overconfident in the world-view, the infrastructure, the detailed management of daily life, which kept us afloat, but perilously neglectful of all that was going on outside or below that apparently subdued and tranquil surface. 'Basking in the moonshine of our collective self-approval', as C. S. Lewis puts it, we could be heading for collision with a perfectly natural iceberg, which we should have detected, assessed, situated and negotiated, if we had been living in the real world that not only surrounds us but actually is us.

Poetry as a personal and private language can be even more pioneering and exploratory in this regard. Ottavio Paz, the recently deceased Mexican writer, who won the Nobel Prize for literature in 1990, wrote a series of 'Essays on Modern Poetry' called *The Other Voice:*

> That voice was not heeded by the revolutionary ideologues of our century, and this explains, in part at least, the cataclysmic failure of their plans. It would be disastrous if the new political philosophy were to ignore those realities that have been hidden and buried by the men and women of the

Modern Age. The function of poetry for the last two hundred years has been to remind us of their existence; the poetry of tomorrow cannot do otherwise. Its mission will not be to provide new ideas but to announce what has been obstinately forgotten for centuries. Poetry is memory become image, and image become voice.[20]

What he is talking about is a universal phenomenon. In Nigeria, for instance, Gabriel Okara's novel, *The Voice,* tells the same story in terms of his River State village. It is to do with individuality, which differentiates itself and thereby delineates itself, because it finds itself being suffocated in the self-definition of the group. 'We are like this, we do things this way, we never say, do, think other than in the prescribed fashion,' the voice of our education constantly reminds us. Poetry, as 'the other voice', speaks for the deeply personal, giving a warm, intuitive affirmation of who and what an individual really is. 'The body heat of poetry, its warm breath', as Heaney describes it, 'keeps stirring the feather of our instinctive nature.'[21] It chimes against the dominant voice of cool, authoritative, scientific, orderly, critical and calculating common sense.

'The poet is occupied with frontiers of consciousness beyond which words fail, though meaning still exists,' T. S. Eliot suggests. Such a poem is a stab at the truth, a touch-stone, a marker, 'an active principle in the reader's consciousness henceforward,' in the words of the American poet, Hart Crane.

Many have taken upon themselves the task of explaining and regulating the mystery of human life, few have had the opportunity of putting their ideas into practice. Situations such as the French Revolution, the American Declaration of Independence and the history of Russia since 1917, have provided scope and opportunity for the implementation of such ideologies. Our own situation in the Irish Republic – whatever one might feel or believe about its justification, its credibility or its ultimate viability – did provide, for those responsible for constituting it, a unique and enviable opportunity to establish a cherishing and vitalising environment for a manageable population on a relatively small-scale. The questions now are: to what extent did they allow what we are here referring to as 'the other voice' to influence their architecture? And the answer to the question is very little if any at all. I am sure we have to say that in the various realms of exploration in the name of humanity, whether it be religion, art or science, there were, at the beginning of this century, many very arrogant, many very fearful and many very well-meaningly belligerent defenders of their own points of view. But there is no doubt that their attitudes and the resulting cold-war and siege mentality have been detrimental to spiritual progress and refinement in all of us.

In Ireland, art as the 'other voice' has been constant and assiduous in attempting to formulate a different, wider, less banal and more variegated identity than the one being prescribed for us by both Church and State. And the relationship between these two voices has not been very harmonious to say the least. Far from the kind of dialogue between our society and the arts that would have been both salutary and envigorating, there developed an atmosphere of fear and suspicion, which was expressed and enshrined in the Censorship Act of 1929. The answer to creative interrogation and criticism on the part of artists was to silence them. Many artists protested vigorously against this Act, perhaps none more eloquently than George Bernard Shaw:

> In the nineteenth century all the world was concerned about Ireland. In the twentieth, nobody outside Ireland cares twopence what happens to her ... If, having broken England's grip of her, she slops back into the Atlantic as a little grass patch in which a few million moral cowards are not allowed to call their souls their own by a handful of morbid Catholics, mad with heresyphobia, unnaturally combining with a handful of Calvanists mad with sexphobia ... then the world will let 'these Irish' go their way into insignificance without the smallest concern.[22]

This situation developed mainly because the Church was identified with the hierarchy and the moral majority, the voice of the Minotaur.

The message of the artists to us, since the beginning of this century, has been pretty consistent as I read it, and has been stubbornly repudiated or ignored by officialdom both in the Church and in the State. And the message is this: the picture of humanity that you are painting, whether in its ideal form or in your perception of what it is actually like, is too narrow, too pessimistic, too 'other-wordly,' too unsubtle. You refuse to accept the blood-and-guts reality of what we are, the bodily, sexual, earthy almagam that makes us who we are. The French philosopher Lachelier is supposed to have woken up one morning at the age of twenty-six, saying to himself: 'This morning I realize that I am the son of a man and a woman; that disappoints me: I thought I was a little more than that.' We don't want to be more than that. We want to be human, fully human. We believe that God so loved our humanity that he sent his only son to share it with us and to make it part of his life. You are trying to deny that reality, trying to create your own picture of what that humanity should be like if it is to be worthy of such relationship. We say No. If God doesn't want our humanity the way it is, the way he made it, then he doesn't want us at all. He wants something else. The job of the artist is to describe and express that reality as it actually is. Artists have been doing that from the beginning of this century, especially in Ireland, and because they have been doing precisely that they have been condemned, banned, excommunicated by the official organs of the Church.

James Joyce was a religious man. He wasn't an atheist. He believed that the humanity being presented, endorsed, canonised by the church was a fake. He gave his life and his work to defending the orthodoxy of humanity. In a letter to Stanislaus, his brother, in 1906 Joyce says: 'If I put a bucket into my own soul's well, sexual department, I draw up Griffith's and Ibsen's and Skeffington's and Bernard Vaughan's and St. Aloysius' and Shelley's and Renan's water along with my own. And I am going to do that in my novel (*inter alia*) and plank the bucket down before the shades and substances above mentioned to see how they like it: and if they don't like it I can't help them. I am nauseated by their lying drivel about pure men and pure women and spiritual love for ever: blatant lying in the face of the truth.'[23]

Unlike Milton, whose self-professed purpose was to describe the ways of God to humankind, Joyce wanted to describe as accurately as he knew how the ways of humankind to God. Rilke, Joyce's contemporary, made a similar protest:

> Why, I ask you, when people want to help us, who are so often helpless, why do they leave us in the lurch just there at the root of all experience? Anyone who would stand by us there could rest satisfied that we should ask nothing further from him. For the help which he imparted to us there would grow of itself with our life, becoming, together with it, greater and stronger. And would never fail. Why are we not set in the midst of what is most mysteriously ours? How we have to creep round about it and get into it in the end; like burglars and thieves, we get into our own beautiful sex, in which we lose our way and knock ourselves and stumble and finally rush out of it again, like men caught transgressing ... Why, if guilt or sin had to be invented because of the inner tension of the spirit, why did they not attach it to some other part of the body, why did they let it fall on that part, waiting until it dissolved in our pure source and poisoned and muddied it? Why have they made our sex homeless, instead of making it the place for the festival of our competency? Why do we not belong to God from this point? My sex is not directed only towards posterity, it is the secret of my own life – and it is only because it may not occupy the central place there, that so many people have thrust it to the edge, and thereby lost their balance.[24]

Throughout this century in Ireland we have been told the same thing in different ways, by Edna O'Brien and John McGahern, for instance. None of these are saying that there is no God, there is no Church, there is no Christianity. On the contrary, they are suggesting that if any of these realities want to have some effective contact with us and operate any kind of comprehensive salvation, they must begin taking seriously the partner with whom they are trying to have such a relationship.

When Sinéad O'Connor tears up publicly a picture of the Pope, it is not because she is an atheist or because she doesn't believe in the Church. It is an act of frustration and disappointment at a particular presentation of the Church and its failure to speak to the kind of people we really are, the kind of people who we have painstakingly become and who we are not prepared to renounce or to betray. In a newspaper interview she says: 'I've always been a religious person ... I consider myself to be a Christian person ... I also believe that out of all this there'll probably end up being a very good Church ... a good healthy church that's doing its job ... If you deny sexuality then you deny God ... So how can you expect priests not to be sexually abusive if they have to deny their sexuality or believe that there's something wrong with it? ... So once they let women in – which I'm sure they will eventually – I reckon they'll have a really united Church that'll be an inspiration to the rest of the world.'[25]

When I read Roddy Doyle's *The Snapper* I cried with laughter not just because it is so funny but because it is so true. This is accurate cardiography of the present-day heartbeat. And it is too bad if the Magisterium of the Catholic Church is disapproving, is saying no, you've got to change all that, you've got to go back to what we were like in the 1940s. We are not going back. And anyway the 1940s were nothing like you are pretending they were. Read *Angela's Ashes*.[26] They were terrible times for most people, and those who were pretending to be upright and virtuous according to your standards have all too recently been shown, for the most part, to be hypocritical and pathetically incapable of self-control. Your so-called virtue was in such cases simply impotence or incapacity to accede to any kind of virtue whatsoever.

Such, as I understand it, would be the case made by artists in this century against the Church. The viewpoint of the Church that they find unacceptable is derived, also in my view, from a view of human nature, of natural law, and of the prescriptive and omniscient role and mandate of the Church's Magisterium not only in matters of faith but also in the realms of morality and socio-political activity. It seems to me that a different kind of guidance and guardianship should dictate the Church's role in the latter two areas to that which determines its mandate in the area of faith.

If we are to move forward towards a development that respects all the elements in the amalgam that we are, that we have become, that we hope to direct towards the most optimistic future, it is essential that the Church collaborates with scientists and artists who are the antennae, the diviners, the creators of our future. They are our eyes, our ears, our imaginations. Listen to Seamus Heaney in 1991:

> My language and my sensibility is yearning to admit a kind of religious or transcendental dimension. But then there's the reality ... the complacency and the utter simplification of these things into social instructions. That's what's disappointing.[27]

Artists shake our complacency and refuse 'the utter simplification of these things into social instructions.' One of the tasks of poetry, Heaney reminded us in his T. S. Eliot Memorial Lectures of 1986, is to resist moral cowardice. He uses examples of poets in communist states in Eastern Europe who, until quite recently, were living in situations where art was either harnessed to government policy or else became a public enemy of state legislature and ideology. But most of us can recognize the world he is describing:

> A world where poetry is required to take a position that is secondary to religious truth or state security or public order... In ideal republics, Soviet republics, in the Vatican and Bible-belt, it is common expectation that the writer will sign over his or her individual, venturesome and potentially disruptive

activity into the keeping of an official doctrine, a traditional system, a party line.[28]

Nor do we have to be governed by a bloody dictator to undergo such doctrinaire browbeating. Heaney is aware of the Minotaur. 'I am thinking, he says, not so much of authoritarian censorship as of an implacable consensus.' The role of the poet is to expose 'to the majority the abjectness of their collapse, as they flee for security into whatever self-deceptions the party line requires of them.' Like Cézanne at the beginning of the century, Heaney has been trying to show us how to see, how to 'credit marvels' and balance *The Spirit Level.* His poetry and his criticism should become an essential part of the probing that determines the direction we now want to take. Artists are like scouts in the evolutionary march. Their work is to explore the territory ahead and advise on the paths to be tested. Nor is it enough to say 'artists' and 'scientists' without reservation or discrimination. There is an ethic for artists also, without obedience to which they become sterile or mediocre, greedy or irresponsible. There are good and bad artists just as there are good and bad bishops, good and bad scientists.

It seems to me that this was the subject of Brian Friel's last play, *Give Me Your Answer Do.* Friel, let us remember, began his life on the road to priesthood. He left Maynooth after two years in the national seminary in the 1940s, where 'he explored the vocation which he believed he had for the priesthood.'[29] He later said in 1972, when he was forty-three years of age: 'I hope that between now and my death I will have acquired a religion, a philosophy, a sense of life, that will make the end less frightening than it appears to me at this moment.'[30]

The job of articulating just such a philosophy is partly the artist's, and Friel muses aloud about the possibility that our artists at this important time may have sold their integrity to the highest bidder instead of 'fashioning a conscience for their race.' Because, above all, it seems to me, what artists are saying to the Church is this: There *are* truths that are absolute, there are dogmas that have to be preserved and written in stone in credal formulae and liturgical rites, but these are about the interventions of God among us. The truth about human being, especially in relationship, is not such a truth. It cannot be captured in a formula. Art is the only medium subtle enough to express it.

And at this level, at this moment of difficulty and discovery, the role of the hierarchy in the Church might well be to discern rather than to dictate, to peruse rather than prescribe, to exercise their authority and responsibility in a more passive way, by examining the evidence produced and expressed by the scouts and the spies, before endorsing the strategy and confirming the direction that will lead us into the twenty-first century.

# CHAPTER NINE

# THE MINOTAUR

At the centre of the labyrinth, maintaining its legitimacy, is that anonymous creature with the body of a human and the head of a bull. It has no name, nor can it be identified with any particular persons, organisations or power structures. Just as our particular labyrinth is housed within our society, our families, our educational system and even within our own internal psychic structure as individuals who have been educated by and within our own culture, so too the Minotaur is an all-pervasive presence extending its thraldom to the internalised consciousness of each one of us. It is, within this configuration of the myth, the body of public opinion that raises its ugly head whenever any attempt is made either to describe or to denounce the labyrinthine system that is its home, which it has been created by, and that it is destined to defend. Its head, after all, is the head of a bull, so it does not have that human capacity to question fundamentally its natural environment. Instead it defends its nest, its lair, with the same innate savagery and bullheadedness with which any creature of the animal world will obey the dictates of its learned cosmology, and follow the patterns encoded in its cultural skin.

Its language is mob oratory, the roar of the bull. Its rule is maintained by public castigation – even execution if necessary – of dissenting or minority voices, and its authority derives from ritual incantation of religious clichés and traditional shibboleths.

Far from entertaining the possibility that Irish society might contain anachronistic or necrophiliac forces, it proclaims that Ireland is the one country left in the world where the real values of life are endorsed and upheld. In a world of hedonistic consumerism, the Emerald Isle remains an oasis where true spiritual values retain pride of place and the reign of Satan and the spirit of 'the world' are refused their seductive charms. Our little island stands out from the rest as a place where human life is sacred, a place from which, as in the past, the fire of life and love can spread itself, with that missionary zeal that characterises our race, throughout the rest of a world long since sunk into darkness and perdition.

To preserve this 'spiritual' ethos we must rid ourselves of those who might be carriers of the universal disease. Artists, psychologists, commentators are welcome if their purpose is to entertain or confirm us. If, however, their naive and ill-considered purpose is to persuade us of the errors of our ways, then their welcome may be short-lived.

The Minotaur is both the producer and the product of its own labyrinth. It represents the part in each one of us that has been made aggressive, fearful and censorious by the social forces that stunted our own growth and now, in turn, feels threatened and provoked by signs or possibilities of a vitality that is now beyond us.

When these parts join forces and become the voice of 'public opinion', then this internalised superego receives convincing support from the volume and stridency of its own voice, multiplied by the thousands of others echoing the same hostility towards change of any kind. Such a phenomenon has no particular religious denominational affiliation. Its genesis is wider and deeper than any particular religious grouping. The Minotaur of public opinion, the moral majority, is almost identical in proportion, volume, and tactical strategy, whether in the North or in the South of this country for instance.

Drama, as its name implies, is one of the art forms that causes the most controversy, because it is performed in public and can be victimised by immediate atavistic emotional reaction. I want to give a few examples to trace this history, to illustrate the role that art can play in such circumstances, and to show a journey of identity crisis which the theatre in this country has both chronicled and inspired.

I begin on St Valentine's day in 1895 with the opening night of *The Importance of Being Earnest* by Oscar Wilde. Most of his dramas were comedies that camouflaged the devastating seriousness of their intent. It is with hindsight that we can recognize the identity crisis with which Wilde was struggling in this play. Its dedication to Robert Ross points up the sexual identity crisis that haunted Wilde. Earnest not only means what it says, namely being deadly serious and full of good zeal, it is also a Christian name, and, apparently, a code name for homosexuals. That it was performed in London to an ecstatic audience of British high society highlights the socio-political identity crisis of the young Irish artist. At the surface level of the bejewelled passengers in the first class compartments of the *Titanic*, it was hailed as a triumph of witty social repartee; at the level of the iceberg it was social revolution.

Let us listen once again to the famous passage where Mr Worthing is being interviewed by Lady Bracknell as a 'worthy' candidate to marry into her family. Worthing can be sliced into 'worth' and 'thing'. By the end of this interview it is clear that Earnest, because of who and what he is, is a worthless thing. Who you are and what you are are not as important as who and what you are perceived to be by the people who matter, by the moral majority, by fashionable society.

> **Lady Bracknell** [*pencil and note-book in hand*] : I feel bound to tell you that you are not down on my list of eligible young men, although I have the same list as the Dear Duchess of Bolton has. We work together, in fact. However, I am quite ready to enter your name, should your answers be what a really affectionate mother requires … What is your income?
> **Jack:** Between seven and eight thousand a year.
> **Lady Bracknell** [*makes a note in her book*]: In land, or investments?

**Jack:** In investments, chiefly.

**Lady Bracknell:** That is satisfactory. Land has ceased to be either a profit or a pleasure. It gives one position, and prevents one from keeping it up. That's all that can be said about land.

**Jack:** I have a country house with some land, of course, attached to it, about fifteen hundred acres, I believe; but I don't depend on that for my real income.

**Lady Bracknell:** A country house! How many bedrooms? Well, that point can be cleared up afterwards. You have a town house, I hope? A girl with a simple unspoiled nature, like Gwendolen, could hardly be expected to reside in the country.

**Jack:** Well, I own a house in Belgrave square, but it is let by the year to Lady Bloxham. Of course, I can get it back whenever I like, at six month's notice.

**Lady Bracknell:** Lady Bloxham? I don't know her ... What number in Belgrave Square?

**Jack:** 149.

**Lady Bracknell** [*shaking her head*]: The unfashionable side. I thought there was something. However, that could easily be altered.

**Jack:** Do you mean the fashion, or the side?

**Lady Bracknell** [*sternly*]: Both, if necessary, I presume. Now to minor matters. Are your parents living?

**Jack:** I have lost both my parents.

**Lady Bracknell:** To lose one parent, Mr Worthing, may be regarded as a misfortune; to lose both looks like carelessness. Who was your father? He was evidently a man of some wealth.

**Jack:** I am afraid I really don't know. The fact is, Lady Bracknell, I said I had lost my parents. It would be nearer the truth to say that my parents seem to have lost me ... I don't actually know who I am by birth. I was ... well, I was found.

**Lady Bracknell:** Found!

**Jack:** The late Mr Thomas Cardew, an old gentleman of very charitable and kindly disposition, found me, and gave me the name of Worthing, because he happened to have a first-class ticket for Worthing in his pocket at the time. Worthing is a place in Sussex. It is a seaside resort.

**Lady Bracknell:** Where did the charitable gentleman who had a first-class ticket for this seaside resort find you?

**Jack** [*gravely*]: In a hand-bag.

**Lady Bracknell:** A hand-bag?

**Jack** [*very seriously*]: Yes, Lady Bracknell. I was in a hand-bag – a somewhat large, black leather hand-bag, with handles to it – an ordinary hand-bag in fact.

**Lady Bracknell:** In what locality did this Mr James, or Thomas, Cardew come across this ordinary hand-bag?

**Jack:** In the cloak-room at Victoria Station. It was given to him in mistake for his own.

**Lady Bracknell:** The cloak-room at Victoria Station?

**Jack:** Yes. The Brighton line.

**Lady Bracknell:** The line is immaterial. Mr Worthing, I confess I feel somewhat bewildered by what you have just told me. To be born, or at any rate bred, in a hand-bag, whether it had handles or not, seems to me to display a contempt for the ordinary decencies of family life that reminds one of the worst excesses of the French Revolution. And I presume you know what that unfortunate movement led to? As for the particular locality in which the hand-bag was found, a cloak-room at a railway station … could hardly be regarded as an assured basis for a recognized position in good society.

**Jack:** May I ask you what you would advise me to do? I need hardly say I would do anything in the world to ensure Gwendolen's happiness.

**Lady Bracknell:** I would strongly advise you, Mr Worthing, to try and acquire some relations as soon as possible, and to make a definite effort to produce at any rate one parent, of either sex, before the season is quite over.

**Jack:** Well, I don't see how I could possibly manage to do that. I can produce the hand-bag at any moment. It is in my dressing-room at home. I really think that should satisfy you, Lady Bracknell.

**Lady Bracknell:** Me, sir! What has it to do with me? You can hardly imagine that I and Lord Bracknell would dream of allowing our only daughter – a girl brought up with the utmost care – to marry into a cloak-room, and form an alliance with a parcel. Good morning, Mr Worthing!

[*Lady Bracknell sweeps out in majestic indignation.*]

There are so many crises of identity 'cloaked' in this hilarious repartee: town and country, side and fashion, parentage and pedigree. But the whip hand is Lady Bracknell's. She is utterly convinced of the rectitude of her vision of what society should be, what fashion is, what eligibility for acceptability entails, what 'decency' means, and what is and is not an assured basis for a recognized position in good society.

I want to move now to 1907 to another play, this time in the Abbey Theatre, Dublin, founded in 1904 by W. B. Yeats and Lady Gregory, to make sure that Irish artists need never again go to London to stage their genius. After the first night of *The Playboy of the Western World* by J. M. Synge there were riots. To paraphrase Yeats's account of the incident, on the Monday night following, no word of the play was heard from beginning to end, because about forty young men sat in the front seats of the pit and stamped and shouted and blew trumpets all through the performance.

They were protesting against this portrayal of Irish people and wished to silence the slander upon Ireland's womanhood. Irish women would never sleep under the same roof with a young man without a chaperon, nor would they ever use the word 'shift'. How could they recognize the country men and women of Davis and Kickham in these violent grotesques who used the name of God so freely?

Two interesting quotes from Synge: 'A young doctor has just told me that he can hardly keep himself from jumping on to a seat and pointing out in that howling mob those whom he is treating for venereal disease.' And: 'In writing *The Playboy of the Western World,* as in my other plays, I have used one or two words only that I have not heard among the country people of Ireland.' In other words, his genius as artist is to represent the reality of Irish people as they are and as they express themselves. However, for the howling mob in the audience such a representation of who they are is unacceptable. Admittedly both the side and the fashion had changed, but the Minotaur retains the same implacable, self-righteous, condemnatory voice.

In 1918, Brinsley MacNamara published *The Valley of the Squinting Windows,* which was almost a description of the Minotaur in its local habitat. It so enraged the people of Delvin in County Westmeath that the book was publicly burnt and the author's father, a local schoolmaster, was boycotted and exiled.

Moving to 1927 and the presentation of *The Plough and the Stars* by Sean O'Casey. Another Abbey riot. This time about the slur on the patriotism of the people of Ireland. By the second night of the play's one-week run, half a dozen women in the pit stamped and hissed at intervals during the performance. By Thursday the republicans were out in force. Sixty-five year-old Maude Gonne was picketing outside the door with a group of Irish Republicans. One of the women demonstrators told O'Casey as he left the theatre that there wasn't a prostitute in Ireland. Yeats stood up on the stage shouting: 'Long live Ireland and Freedom of expression … You have made fools of yourselves again … This play is an apotheosis.' O'Casey had to look up the word and recorded in his autobiography: 'Did these bawling fools think that their shouting would make him docile? He would leave them to their green hills of Holy Ireland.' The Irish Independent declared that 'there are some things that cannot be defended by invoking the name of Art … It is known to every constant patron of the Abbey that in some plays words have been said and things have been shown that would make even a tolerant censor hesitate. Ireland may have sinned, but she has not become pagan.'

In 1942 Eric Cross published *The Tailor and Ansty,* which, again, according to the author and the two people faithfully portrayed, contained nothing in it except 'the fun and talk and the laughter which has gone on for years around this fireside.' Not only was the book banned for being 'in its general tendency indecent' but copies of it were burned publicly. The tailor himself was forced to kneel in his home while the book was burned in front of him by two priests. There was uproar in the senate and in the Dáil, where, Frank O'Connor recorded acidly in his introduction to the book, 'we were all too innocent to anticipate the effect the book would have on Mr de Valera's well-educated government.' 'When I wrote the introduction to the original edition of *The Tailor and Ansty*,' O'Connor continues, 'the models were still alive. They were a remarkable old couple who lived in a tiny cottage on the mountain road up to the lake at Gougane Barra ... Ansty was a beautiful woman who looked like the Muse of Tragedy but talked like a quite different muse ... The tailor spoke beautiful Irish and was like a rural Dr Johnson.'

Eric Cross was so taken by the couple and so fascinated by their wisdom and conversation that he recorded both in this book. The banning of the book had a devastating effect on the old couple, who were at first persecuted and then virtually ostracised and boycotted by their neighbours. The principal spokesman for the Government, a Professor William Magennis of the National University, described by O'Connor as 'a windbag with a nasty streak of malice', dominated the debate. 'The man is sex-obsessed. His wife, Anastasia – called here 'Ansty' – is what in the language of American psychology is called a moron – a person of inferior mental development who may be thirty or forty years of age, but has reached only the mental age of a child of four or five.' It is interesting to note that Magennis saw this publication as a plot to undermine Christianity in this country. Such a campaign had originated in England, according to him, was financed by American money, and was headed up by George Bernard Shaw, among others.

One year later, by 1943, nearly 2,000 books had been banned including Saul Bellow, Faulkner, Graham Greene, Robert Graves,

Hemingway, Isherwood, Alberto Moravia, Nabokov, Proust, Jean-Paul Sartre, Dylan Thomas, H. G. Wells, Emile Zola, to give an international alphabetical sample. Irish authors who were banned, from Liam O'Flaherty in the 1930s to Lee Dunne in the 1970s, included Frank O'Connor himself, the two Nobel Prize winners, Beckett and Shaw, Austin Clarke, Edna and Kate O'Brien, and, of course, Joyce.

In 1945 the organisation called Maria Duce was the vociferous mouthpiece for right-wing Catholic supervision of public morality. However, it was the League of Decency who, in 1957, tried to have *The Rose Tatoo* closed down at The Pike Theatre in Dublin and eventually had its director, Alan Simpson, imprisoned. He was charged with 'producing for gain an indecent and profane performance.'

Two and a half years later *The Ginger Man* by J. P. Donleavy had to be closed after three performances at the Gaiety because of indecent and obscene references which the author refused to cut.

The 1971 film *Ryan's Daughter,* written by Robert Bolt and David Lean and based on Flaubert's *Madame Bovary,* received the following notice in The National Film Institute's report: 'When for the production of this film Lean sought period German weapons from the Irish Army authorities, he bolstered his request with a letter from a retired army colonel to the effect that there was nothing in the script to portray the Irish in an unfavourable light … The portrayal of the village idiot by Mills is as disgusting and as nauseating as his acting is excellent. The part played by Sarah Miles – the local publican's daughter – the village beauty, shows the Irish country girls in a disgustingly immoral light … A film with little theme, with little regard for the true situation of the 1916 period.' It's the same accusation all the time: slanders about our sexual mores and innuendoes about the purity of our nationalist intent.

By now we were into the television era. When, in 1977, Tom Murphy's *The White House* was screened by RTÉ it met a response described by Fintan O'Toole as 'the modern equivalent of the riots which greeted *The Playboy of the Western World* and *The Plough and the Stars*'. It elicited a resolution from the Youghal Urban Council protesting against 'the scandalous filth of RTE programmes'. Tipperary North Riding Council called it 'scurrilous and filthy'. The West Donegal executive of Fine Gael condemned it as a 'blasphemy' and 'a gross insult to Christian principles'. In Cashel it was condemned by both Protestant and Catholic clergy. Cork County Council regarded the play as 'obscene' and 'absolutely disgraceful' and it was attacked in an editorial in *The Cork Examiner*.

What are all these explosive, antagonistic and negative reactions for the most part? They come from a fearful protective mechanism which hides the ambiguity, the treachery, the 'evil' inside ourselves. This works by constructing a corresponding hate object outside ourselves on which we can exorcise our panic and insecurity. We have an idealised version of ourselves and anything other than this is repressed. However, it continues to prowl the depths. Projection is the term used for throwing all the contents of that shadow onto someone else. We see and condemn in the monster outside all those weaknesses and tendencies that we fail to acknowledge or accept inside ourselves. In the Irish Catholic psyche such hate objects or scape-goats, upon which it was acceptable, even encouraged, to expend any amount of hatred were, for instance, Oliver Cromwell, Judas Iscariot, and Satan. These were the enlarged caricatures, the projected parasites, of the repressed side of ourselves, what Brian Friel called *The Enemy Within* in his play about St Columba, the archetypal paragon of Irish virtue.

We have an idealised version of ourselves as we should be and Columba is one of the role models for such perfection. The rest is repressed. Such repression is more than suppression. It is more than denying or controlling urges or impulses that we actually feel in ourselves. *Repression is refusing even to acknowledge the existence of such realities.* The mere entertainment of them would be too shameful to tolerate with self respect. Repression pushes even the memory of such thoughts and feelings into oblivion. An unmarried person, for instance, who believes that any thought of sexual intercourse outside of marriage is immoral may repress these sexual urges consciously until they are seemingly obliterated. However, at the unconscious level they continue to live a life of their own, which may manifest itself in hysterical condemnation of sexual indulgence in others. This sanitising process, whereby people wipe out everything that is deemed unworthy of a human being, leads to condemnation of others who fail to achieve this goal. Their particular definition of sanity, the sane society, dictates that they label 'insane' and commit to a safe asylum whoever fails to reach their required standards. Artists and others whose way of life appears to them to be either outlandish or unacceptable are often vulnerable targets. The Minotaur, in its role as champion of the voice of sanity, is quick to pronounce a verdict of insanity on all those whose behaviour falls outside the prescribed norms.

# ART AND INSANITY

The late Dr Soedjatmoko who was rector of the United Nations University in Tokyo, addressing a conference of the World Federation for Mental Health in Washington in the summer of 1983, suggested that our world was entering a period in its history when it would almost inevitably behave like a mentally ill patient. The two main causes for this would be 'rapid, fundamental and unprecedented social and value changes throughout the world' and the strain upon our adjustment capacity effected by major scientific and technological advances.

Many experts and professionals dealing with the mentally ill make a distinction between those who are normal, those who are neurotic and those who are psychotic. There is an important hiatus between each category and yet all three belong to a continuum. The differences are quantitative rather than qualitative. Every one of us inhabits a dream world at night-time, whether we are aware of this or not. We know of research conducted during times of war, and under controlled experimentation at other times, when people for various reasons have been prevented from sleeping. Such deprivation produces psychotic states because the salutary possibility of inhabiting dreamtime is withheld. In other words, most of us are mildly schizoid by night and this abnormality is what keeps us sane during the day. Normality, neurosis, psychosis are expressions, at different levels of intensity and in differing degrees of concentration, of our common psychosomatic make-up. Every neurosis and every psychosis is inherent in each of us potentially. An understanding of what such states might be can be gained by listening to those who have been through them or are going through them. This is vitally important if, as has been suggested, more and more people are going to be entering such states and we may all be heading in that direction in the near future. Both Freud and Jung were forever at loggerheads with their professional contemporaries on this point. They wanted to introduce psychodynamic psychology into psychiatry and to treat various mental illnesses psychotherapeutically. In his time, Jung tells us, 'Schizophrenia was considered incurable. If one did achieve some improvement with a case of schizophrenia, the answer was that it had not been real schizophrenia.' He records that 'through my work with patients I realised that paranoid ideas and hallucinations contain a germ of meaning. A personality, a life history, a pattern of hopes and desires lie behind the psychosis. The fault is ours if we do not understand them. It dawned upon me then for the first time that a general psychology of the personality lies concealed within psychosis ... Although patients may appear ... totally imbecillic, there is more going on in their minds, and more that is meaningful, than there seems to be. At bottom we discover nothing new and unknown in the mentally ill; rather, we encounter the substratum of their own natures.'[31]

At the outset, it needs to be said that neither Jung, nor indeed I, would wish to underestimate or romanticise the horror of psychotic breakdown. On the contrary, it is the recognition of such hell that spurs us on to discover a new route to and from such territories. The suggestion I am making is that, of all the categories of human beings who have suffered mental illness of whatever kind, artists are the ones most likely to be able to offer us some coherent insight into what they have been through, or of what their illness is about. Not only that. Artists may be the forerunners of precisely the kind of mental illness that is already erupting and going to affect society as a whole in later times. They are like highly sensitive animals whose antennae can detect, and who feel in their bones, the storm clouds which are not yet visible or apparent to the rest of us, but which will become all too obvious when the storm itself is later unleashed. Once again Jung was aware of this possibility: 'What the artist and the insane have in common is common also to every human being – a restless creative fantasy which is constantly engaged in smoothing away the hard edges of reality ... We healthy people, who stand with both feet in reality, see only the ruin of the patient in this world, but not the richness of that side of the psyche which is turned away from us. Unfortunately only too often no further knowledge reaches us of the things that are being played out on the dark side of the soul, because all the bridges have broken down which connect that side with this ... In insanity we ... are looking at the foundations of our own being, the matrix of those vital problems on which we are all engaged.'[32]

Two artists, Vincent van Gogh (1853-1890) and Gustave Flaubert (1821-1880), almost contemporaries one hundred years ago, represent the two possibilities about art and artists which I am trying to present, and which find themselves validated in our experience a century later. Listen to Vincent writing to his brother Theo, the year before his death (3 February 1889):[33] 'But as for considering myself as completely sane, we must not do it. People here who have been ill like me have told me the truth. You may be old or young, but there will always be moments when you lose your head.' Van Gogh was perceived to be mad and was locked up in an asylum at the explicit request of his neighbours. He himself knew that what they called 'madness' was really his own attempt to reach the truth about himself in the deepest recesses of his being, which was also the truth about his neighbours. He had written to Theo some years earlier (October 1883): 'They said I was out of my mind, but I knew myself that it was not true, for the very reason that I felt my own disease deep within me, and tried to remedy it. I exhausted myself in hopeless unsuccessful efforts, it is true, but because of that fixed idea of reaching a normal point of view again, I never mistook my own desperate doings, worryings and drudgings for my real innermost self.' Van Gogh left behind at least forty-three portraits of himself as witnesses to the fact that he was not 'mad', and as introductions to himself as he really was. For him self-portraiture was the struggle to 'remain human' in a society hostile both to himself and to the arts. 'I should like to paint portraits', he writes to Willemien in 1890, 'which would appear after a century to the people living then as apparitions.'

Van Gogh's wonderfully moving face bears witness to us, the people living a century later, to a loneliness and a sense of failure of a misunderstood genius, at the end of the century in which he had to live. How many people today at the end of our century does he represent? A year before he shot himself in despair, he wrote to Theo (19 June 1889): 'Unfortunately we suffer from the circumstances and the ills of the times in which we live, for better or for worse.' And in September of that same year before he died, he again wrote to his brother: 'I with my mental disease, I keep thinking of so many other artists suffering mentally, and I tell myself that this does not prevent one from exercising the painter's profession as if nothing were amiss.'

There are people in America today who, when they die, have their bodies frozen and preserved in a vault at great expense, so that they can be defrosted by a society whose skills in science and medicine will have improved sufficiently to cure them of the diseases from which they died. In a similar but more creative way, Vincent left his self-portraits to a future generation who would have understood him more. He saw himself as 'a link in the chain of artists,' a pathfinder for future generations. He was a selfless worker towards a new society which would be energised and nourished by the arts. About one of these self-portraits, which he dedicated to Gauguin, he wrote: 'There is an art of the future, and it is going to be so lovely and so young that, even if we give up our youth for it, we must gain in serenity.' And which of us can look without some sense of guilt about our so-called sanity at the last self-portrait in unbuttoned coat against a background of rhythmically whirling lines, which now hangs in Paris, but which was painted in Saint-Remy some months before he died. Here is the last look of an artist before he goes into the darkness against which he struggled as a painter for the thirty-seven years of his life. He never sold a single painting during his lifetime, except one to his brother Theo. He had to beg for the money to buy the yellow ochre that he used to paint the picture which a hundred years later was sold in Sotheby's for over £6 million sterling. Theo had written to his own wife in 1888 about his brother Vincent: 'If it had been granted to him once to find someone to whom he could pour out his heart, it might never have come to this.'

The two points I wish to draw attention to are: firstly, that mental illness can be the result of obdurate and blind circumstances surrounding sensitivity and search for identity; and, secondly, that art can be the way forward towards a more comprehensive and subtle understanding of the human psyche.

Flaubert illustrates this suggestion very graphically. When he finished writing *Madame Bovary* in 1855, it appeared to the society in which he lived as an unbelievably scandalous account of the inner workings of a young married woman's mind. It was read as an outrage to public morality, it was condemned as obscene and insane. More recent critics criticize the author for presuming to understand the mind of a woman in love. The answer to this second criticism is Flaubert's famous riposte: '*Madame Bovary, c'est moi*,' showing the continuity of that spectrum which we all inhabit as male and female.

What was an isolated phenomenon in a scandalous novel a hundred years ago became the condition of a whole generation, when France of the 1960s was diagnosed as having '*le bovarysme*' (here comes everybody as Madame Bovary) a 'disease' that came to a head in the May revolution of 1968. Whether the artist invents a mental state that later generations assume by osmosis, imitation or conviction, or whether the artist is aware of – or becomes possessed by – something that lies incubating at the heart of each one of us, there is a 'prophetic' quality about works of art, especially works created by those deemed by their contemporaries to be insane.

Marcel Proust (1871-1922) and Franz Kafka (1883-1924) bring us interesting evidence from the dawn of our own century. In an essay called 'The Sanity of True Genius', Anthony Storr, the psychiatrist, psychotherapist and writer, sums up his argument as follows:

> 'Men and women who are creatively gifted are characterized by a susceptibility to mental illness which is greater than average but which does not necessarily lead to actual breakdown because creative powers are to some extent protective against mental illness ... It has been demonstrated that creative people exhibit more neurotic traits than the average person, but are also better equipped than most people to deal with their neurotic problems. It has also been shown that some of the psychological characteristics which are inherited as part of the predisposition to schizophrenia are divergent, loosely associative styles of thinking which, when normal, are 'creative', but which, when out of control, are transformed into the 'thought disorder' typical of schizophrenia'.[34]

In Proust and Kafka we have two artists who seem to have elucidated the psychotic state of the twentieth century in works of art which are uncanny in their prefiguration of the history that later unfolded – history not just of individuals suffering from particular kinds of derangement but also in the larger canvas of totalitarian government with its oppressive effect upon individuals, minorities, ethnic groups and social classes. Kafka's *The Trial*, *The Castle*, and some of his short stories have been seen as prophetic foretellings of the horrors of later happenings in Germany, Russia and China, with all the techniques to obtain confessions from prisoners used by interrogators in many twentieth-century regimes. In fact, for Kafka, it all boiled down to one particularly sensitive child's relationship with an overbearing, whimsical and bullying father. In *The Trial*, Josef K. imagines his persecutors as 'two giants of enormous size [who] were bargaining above his head for himself'. Storr points out that this is the view-point of a child in an adult world. Here it is of interest to note Lacan's theory that 'in the majority of neuroses of our time we can designate the principal determinant in the personality of the father who is always lacking in some way or other.'[35] In his famous 'Letter to His Father', Kafka himself makes clear that whatever the actual reality of his real father's temperament and psychology, the effect that this particular parent had upon a highly precocious and sensitive son was to induce what can only be described as ontological insecurity, a complete lack of identity, a fear that his own inherent worthlessness and loathsomeness made him not only completely disposable but likely to be disposed of at whim. He identifies one particular moment as a child in bed at night asking for water, when his father picked him up and put him out on the balcony. This incident was the catalyst and the symbol of the 'sense of nothingness' which his father induced in him: 'Even years afterwards I suffered from the tormenting fancy that the huge man, my father, the ultimate authority, would come almost for no reason at all and take me out of bed in the night and carry me out on to the pavlatche [balcony] and that therefore I was a mere nothing for him.'[36]

Kafka's 'art' is the articulation of fears which 'lurk in the recesses of the mind in all of us, but which, in the ordinary course of events, only become manifest in those whom we label 'psychiatric patients.'[37] Kafka carried from his childhood into adult life a crushing and oppressive feeling of always being at the mercy of other people, of being a victim, of being barely tolerated, of not being worthy of existence. His works are laden with sado-masochistic fantasies and he exemplifies what Storr calls 'the schizoid dilemma: a desperate need for love nullified by an equally desperate fear of actual proximity.'[38]

This hiatus is perfectly spanned by his writing, which allowed him both to express himself without need for involvement with others and also to exorcise the demons of his childhood. So, his art is both the result and the expression of his mental illness, as well as being symptomatic of the illness of a new generation, whose psychosis has been played out for us in so many versions and scenarios.

If Kafka is the artist who plays out the motifs of our most obvious catalyst for psychosis, the relationship with the father, Proust's life and work was a struggle with the other possibility, the relationship with the mother. As with Kafka, this obsession is crystallized in one biographical moment which is almost parallel. The six-year-old Proust is also lying in bed in the dark waiting for his mother to come to give him a goodnight kiss. She fails to turn up because she has guests and this most sensitive of spurned lovers becomes aware at that precise moment of what each one of us becomes aware of in whatever way or to whatever degree our coarser sensitivities may register, 'that love is doomed and happiness does not exist.' This is one of the other great sources of neurotic paralysis and psychotic behaviour. But it remains deeply embedded in the unconscious for most of us and remains there as a largely undisturbed wreck which constantly influences the apparent surface calmness of our workaday lives. Proust made it his business to dive down to this wreck and develop for himself the techniques and the musculature that would allow him singlehandedly to haul it up to the surface and plonk it there as an ungainsayable monster before our eyes. Part of this effort on his part required some obnoxious acts of cruelty which he performed himself on live rats. His tapping into the unconscious was no ordinary work of memory. It required 'the past brought to life in an odour or a sight which it causes to explode.'[39] His biographer tells us that 'he was performing symbolic acts of revenge for an injury inflicted in remote childhood, perhaps even further back than the kiss refused and extorted on the moonlight night at Auteuil. It was when he was only twenty-two months old, and his brother Robert was born, that it became forever impossible for him to possess his mother's undivided love.'[40]

Jung was probably the first to call Joyce a prophet.[41] 'There are', he says, 'major and minor prophets, and history will decide to which of them Joyce belongs. Like every true prophet, the artist is the unwitting mouth-piece of the psychic secrets of his time, and is often as unconscious as a sleep-walker. He supposes that it is he who speaks, but the spirit of the age is his prompter, and whatever this spirit says is proved true by its effects.' The other controversial statement that Jung made about Joyce was that, like Picasso, he was schizophrenic. This second remark caused such a furore that Jung had to explain himself in 1934 in a footnote: 'By this I do not mean ... a diagnosis of the mental illness schizophrenia ... but a disposition or habitus on the basis of which a serious psychological disturbance could produce schizophrenia. Hence I regard neither Picasso nor Joyce as psychotics.'[42]

To my mind the two statements are connected and, in Joyce's case, the schizophrenic gave birth to the prophet. The etymology of schizophrenia describes a cleavage of the mind and a disconnection between thoughts, feelings and actions. That Joyce was temperamentally prone to this reaction is probably best illustrated by the fact that his daughter, Lucia, was in fact diagnosed on 29 May 1931 as suffering from hebephrenic psychosis, which is a form of schizophrenia characterised by hallucinations, absurd delusions, silly mannerisms and other kinds of deterioration.

Joyce refused to accept that there was anything really wrong with Lucia, declaring that if she were insane then so was he. However, his attitude towards medicine and psychoanalysis changed radically when he was faced with the spectacle of his demented daughter. He even agreed to put her under the care of Jung and came to realise that the night-world that he himself was exploring was probably too harsh for ordinary mortals and that the therapeutic and scientific approaches to it, which he had once disdained, were perhaps the only means of access to it for the majority of people. It is interesting to note that the copy of *Ulysses* which was in Jung's library is signed in 1934: 'To Dr. C. G. Jung, with grateful appreciation of his aid and counsel. James Joyce.' Lucia had been under the care of Jung for three months, from 28 September of that same year, when Joyce wrote this dedication. However, Jung was the twentieth doctor to have been consulted and Joyce again refused to accept his verdict and took Lucia back to Paris with him. As a result of this episode, Jung wrote his considered opinion of the two in a letter to Patricia Hutchins:

If you know anything of my Anima theory, Joyce and his daughter are a classical example of it. She was definitely his 'femme inspiratrice', which explains his obstinate reluctance to have her certified. His own Anima, i.e. unconscious psyche, was so solidly identified with her, that to have her certified would have been as much as an admission that he himself had a latent psychosis. It is therefore understandable that he could not give in. His 'psychological' style is definitely schizophrenic, with the difference, however, that the ordinary patient cannot help himself talking and thinking in such a way, while Joyce willed it and moreover developed it with all his creative forces, which incidentally explains why he himself did not go over the border. But his daughter did, because she was no genius like her father, but merely a victim of her disease. In any other time of the past Joyce's work would never have reached the printer, but in our blessed XXth century it is a message, though not yet understood.[43]

Joyce believed that Lucia was a clairvoyante, that her ravings were similar to his language in *Finnegans Wake*, all of which is important as an approach to this work. Whether by disease or natural genius, Joyce was able to situate himself in a psychic dimension, which for others as yet is only available in such unconscious states as sleep, and still retain his consciousness sufficiently to allow expression of this dimension to filter through into a text. Jung calls this 'visceral thinking' (in which case he points to the presiding bodily organs in such episode of *Ulysses* as significant) or 'conversation in and with one's own intestines'[44] which describes a process 'of almost universal "restratification" of modern man, who is in the process of shaking off a world that has become obsolete'.[45]

The whole perspective that governs our world in terms of latitude and longitude, outer and inner, conscious and unconscious, past, present and future, dream and reality, is one that was fashioned by mankind as a spectator to the universe instead of a participator in the universe. The particular gifts of Joyce allowed him to situate himself quite 'naturally' at another place within himself, from which the language of *Finnegans Wake* quite naturally flows. It isn't as if Joyce were 'consciously' trying to be perverse and to write in a way that was deliberately exotic. Joyce said to John Eglinton about the language in *Finnegans Wake*, 'I write in that way because it comes naturally to me to do so'.[46] Writing at this level, and from this level, participates in the real motive force of the universe. It does not just describe the observed causality of the universe, it participates in the psychic dimension of that a-causal connecting principle which is the real motor force of the world. Jung quotes Sir James Jeans as saying that it is possible 'that the springs of events in this substratum include our own mental activities, so that the future course of events may depend in part on these mental activities'.[47]

This would mean that Joyce was a prophet in the very real sense of having tapped the resources of a language that did not content itself merely with describing the causality of the world from a distant and observational point of view, but actively enmeshed itself in the well-springs of such causality. That Joyce, himself, was aware of such a possibility is suggested by his remark to Oscar Schwarz in Trieste, 'My art is not a mirror held up to nature. Nature mirrors my art' and his claim that there were many examples in his work of clairvoyance, where future events had borne out predictions carried in his earlier work. This would mean that Joyce had discovered a language the resources and power of which have not, as yet, been imagined.

*Finnegans Wake* is directly connected to the reality it describes in the same way that the dream is indistinguishable from the world of the unconscious to which it gives expression. Here language is not the translation of a reality into a text, it is the immediate textual gesture of that reality itself. The work of the author of such a text is not that of establishing the causal connection between one word and the next, as if words were cut and dried atoms with a quantified quota of univocal sense. Here the author's job is to find within each word the peculiar gesture of itself that will reveal an unsuspected and hidden meaning, which will, quite by accident, lead on to the next unforeseen gesture of language. 'You may be as practical as is predictable' Shem says of his use of language in *Finnegans Wake*, 'but you must have the proper sort of accident to meet that kind of being with a difference.'[48] This describes the artistic process of *Finnegans Wake*. It is the unconscious as language itself, not the unconscious described by language. The text itself is woven out of the hidden energy sparked off by language whose entirely fortuitous gestures, under the guiding hand of the author, provide a providential similarity of sound or appearance in a word, thus revealing new connections between two or more beings indicated by that word.

Early on in the *Wake*, Joyce advises us to stop if we are 'abcedminded'.[49] Here the use of language is not as an ABC of signifiers that refer to concepts in a shorthand morse code. Language in the *Wake* is a series of gestures of being, and the work of the author is to search for the 'nameform that whets the wits that convey contacts that sweeten sensation that drives desire that adheres to attachment that dogs death that bitches birth that entails the ensuance of existentiality. But with a rush out of his navel reaching the reredos of Ramasbatham'.[50] This is not the language of the conscious mind, it is visceral language that rushes out of the intestines from a nervous substrate like the sympathetic system, which is quite different from the cerebrospinal system, which produces the rational language of ordinary discourse.

Samuel Beckett (1906-1989) is probably one of the most important 'mental' patients of this century, and a spokesperson for the darker side of ourselves. His art, as he says in *Ill seen ill said*, is where 'Imagination at wit's end spreads its sad wings.' Both wit and word are weak, but they are the indispensible tools of his art, which he once described as 'an art of failure… with nothing to express and no means to express it.'[51] Whereas, according to Ellmann,[52] 'Joyce claimed to have given a voice to the third of human life that is spent in sleep, Beckett could claim to have given a voice to the third of every existence likely to be spent in decay.'

He is very near to Proust when he sees the role of the artist as allowing 'being' to enter art by renouncing our particular will to be ourselves and allowing the voices of language to speak. One of his most interesting works from the point of view of ascertaining his own view of art early in his career – he was twenty-five when he published it in 1931 – is his essay on Proust, in which he compares such art to a kind of 'madness.' 'He will write as he has lived – in Time,' he concedes, 'but it is treated with 'pathological power.' 'Proust's chronology is extremely difficult to follow' and his characters and themes 'seem to obey an almost insane inward necessity' because 'the work of art [is] neither created nor chosen, but discovered, excavated, pre-existing within the artist, a law of his nature.' Beckett is reminded of Schopenhauer's definition of the artistic procedure as 'the contemplation of the world independently of the principle of reason', which he translates in the case of Proust's 'impressionism' as 'his non-logical statement of phenomena in the order and exactitude of their perception, before they have been distorted into intelligibility in order to be forced into a chain of cause and effect.' This last description of what he calls 'distortion' is more or less what most of us mean by sanity. 'The Proustian stasis' on the other hand, 'is contemplative, a pure act of understanding', which Beckett describes as madness, although he uses the Latin *amabilis insania* and the German *holder Wahnsinn* to show how beautiful and desirable it is.[53]

Beckett described his guide to Proust as an examination of 'that double-headed monster of damnation and salvation –Time.' This is the monster that produces great works of art and at the same time induces psychosis. But it also explains the essential continuum of the human mind within which both realities are encompassed.

In an interview with Beckett in 1957, Ellmann gleaned the following interpretation of Joyce's interest in this regard. 'Joyce's fictional method does not presume that the artist has any supernatural power, but that he has an insight into the methods and motivations of the universe ... To Joyce reality was a paradigm, an illustration of a possibly unstatable rule. Yet perhaps the rule can be surmised. It is not a perception of order or of love; more humble than either of these, it is a perception of coincidence.'[54] This would correspond almost exactly with Jung's description of a similar preoccupation. In his paper on 'Synchronicity: An A-causal Connecting Principle' he defines this term as 'the parallelism of time and meaning between psychic and psychophysical events, which scientific knowledge so far has been unable to reduce to a common principle. The term explains nothing, it simply formulates the occurrence of meaningful coincidences which, in themselves, are chance happenings, but are so improbable that we must assume them to be based on some kind of principle, or on some property of the empirical world. No reciprocal causal connection can be shown to obtain between parallel events, which is just what gives them their chance character. The only recognizable and demonstrable link between them is a common meaning, or equivalence'.[55]

The 'Scylla and Charybdis' episode of *Ulysses*, which comes under the organ of the brain, is constantly being lowered from the surface level of narrative causality (and all causality is the idiomatic language of the brain) to another level of synchronicity which introduces a dimension outside the space, time and causality of the narrative as such. This echoes the thought of Jung in his essay on synchronicity: 'we must ask ourselves whether there is some other nervous substrate in us, apart from the cerebrum, that can think and perceive, or whether the psychic processes that go on in us during loss of consciousness are synchronistic phenomena, i.e. events that have no causal connection with organic processes.' After a lengthy argument he comes to the conclusion 'that a nervous substrate like the sympathetic system, which is absolutely different from the cerebrospinal system in point of origin and function can evidently produce thoughts and perceptions just as easily as the latter'.[56]

If this third dimension is present in *Ulysses* it is only so as product and not as a total presence. This is why the novel form could not satisfy Joyce. The dimension hinted at in *Ulysses* had to be expressed in a much more positive and immediate way, as presence rather than absence. This takes place in *Finnegans Wake* where Joyce does not content himself with producing the effects of synchronicity within the time-space continuum of a novel but actually works his way back to the a-causal dimension and expresses it directly.

Jung, in his essay, shows what a difficult task such a project is: 'The idea of synchronicity with its inherent quality of meaning produces a picture of the world so irrepresentable as to be completely baffling.'[57]

The dimension from which such communication must occur is no longer the 'day-time' of *Ulysses* but, rather, what Jung refers to as 'a twilight state'.[58] In such a state, Jung wonders whether 'the normal state of unconsciousness in sleep, and the potentially conscious dreams it contains, ... are produced not so much by the activity of the sleeping cortex, as by the unsleeping sympathetic system, and are therefore of a transcerebral nature'.[59]

Such expression would require 'a new conceptual language – a "neutral language" and a modality without a cause which Jung calls a-causal orderedness'. All of this seems appropriate as a description of Joyce's project in *Finnegans Wake*.

Art and artists can be symptomatic expressions of the cultural unconscious and like all symptoms they are effects from which we must learn because they lead to whatever caused them. In most cases they lead to the oldest and deepest stories within ourselves, which we need to listen to. Artists often walk the borderline between neurosis and psychosis. Their art often prevents them from falling over this border, but it is also stimulated by this delicate balance. How do we harness this energy? How do we tap this source without plunging into the hades of psychosis? Again it seems to me that this 'new' language, this a-causal orderedness, which Jung links with synchronicity, can be heard, can be cultivated, can be learned. And I am suggesting that it becomes more and more important to try to do so.

# CHAPTER ELEVEN

# THE POETS AND THE POPE

There are some who would ask what right has art or poetry to speak against truths that have been handed down to us by either God himself or his appointed representatives. The answer is twofold. On the one hand, the Church as it was intended was built on the foundations of the apostles and the prophets. We are inclined to understand these two foundations as one thing and to say this sentence as if it were two ways of saying the same thing. But each of these foundations represents a distinct principle. In the context of our present discussion, the bishop represents the former and the artist the latter.

We are talking about tradition, about the handing on of the truth, the very basis of our belief in Christianity. This word tradition, as has often been pointed out, is the same word in Latin (*tradere*) for handing on, or handing over. It can also be used – and is used in the Gospels – for the handing over of Jesus to the soldiers by Judas, in other words for 'betrayal.' The problem of culture becomes even more acute when we claim that our religion comes from outside ourselves. It is not just our nerves in patterns on a screen. It is divine revelation, God intervening in our lives and invading our cultural cocoon. The problem is this: whether it be true or not, the only way in which it is possible for God to reach us – to speak to us, to touch us, to appear to us – is through our culture and through the human body, which allows anything we are aware of to be mediated to us. And, once this has been done, the only way we have of carrying the message, of recording the event, of reminding ourselves that it happened is, again, through the culture that is so tightly woven around us. Thus, Claudel will say that God speaks in French and the American Indians will say that God is a buffalo, although people of other countries have never seen one. Everything we know has to be recorded through the weak yet indispensable means of communication at our disposal.

This causes two other problems: the first is that God's initial revelation is always like a meteorite that passes clean through the fabric of our world. It 'appears' and someone is aware of it, but they have no idea who it is or what is happening. Later we 'tell' about the burning bush or the angel wrestling with us, but that is the reminiscence after the event, the stones we place around the crater left behind to remind us that God was here, *terrible est locus iste*. But I am as near to the burning bush as Moses was in terms of 'understanding'. In fact I might be nearer than he was at the time because of the panic that must have overcome him when he began to surmise what might be happening. It is after the event that the tribe gathers round and begins to record what happened and to initiate the various strategies that will help them not to forget and ensure that the God who has visited remains a benign presence. So the accounts, the propositions, the rituals, the creeds are all dependent upon, and moulded by, the culture into which the divine visitation has been thrust. And we can never be sure that this cultural overlay has not damaged, distorted, diluted or destroyed the original presence.

Hans Urs Von Balthasar points out that for Christians 'there can have been no witnesses to the event of the Son's Resurrection by the Father – any more than there can to the act of the Incarnation. And yet the two actions are foundational events ...'[60] He goes on:

> The self-disclosure of fundamentally transcendent events vis-
> a-vis witnesses in space and time requires not only that free
> room for manoeuvre which befits the One who reveals

himself, but also free room for interpretation into human words and images, for which the interpreter must take responsibility in his own freedom as well as in the obligation incumbent on him to speak out ... Words, like (scenic) images remain of necessity 'limit-expressions' for a reality which – since it has absorbed in itself in a transcendent way the entire reality of the old aeon – overflows on all sides the latter's receptive capacities. Depending on just how one interprets the concept, one can call the images which contain the 'holy saga' 'mythical' or one can refuse to use that much abused expression and speak rather of the 'need for a work of translation' into 'figural language' in which 'the decision about the choice of appropriate concepts and expressive media ... was already made by the apostles and evangelists.'[61]

So the first half of our problem as Christians is the unbridgeable shadowline between the original manifestation and any records or testimonies that now remain, all of which are irretrievably embedded in the phenomenon of culture. The second half of our problem is to examine the possibility that any one of the various cultural overlays that encrusted this revelation between the time it broke into the world and the time it was transmitted to us could have been corruptive of it.

There have been moments in the history of the Church when the truth was maintained by only one or two people – one or two prophets – all the rest had fled or had betrayed it. Such a moment is recorded in the life of Maximus the Confessor, who alone bore witness to the fundamental truth for all of us, including the three persons of the Trinity, that there were two wills in the person of Jesus Christ, a human will and a divine will. Everyone else in the official Church, including the Pope of the time, was supporting what later became known as the Monothelite heresy, which declared anathema anyone who held that there was more than one will in the person of Jesus Christ. Maximus was martyred by officialdom, had his limbs cut off and his tongue cut out, but he stubbornly maintained what he knew to be true. His protest, his courage, his self-imposed exile from the official Church of his day not only forced that same Church to acknowledge his personal sanctity, but it also ensured that all future officialdom would be obliged to support and uphold the point of view that he so stubbornly and singlehandedly refused to abandon. And his point was quite simply this: there is never – never has been nor ever can be – a situation where God takes over the human will of some individual person and dictates His will through their mouths, their fingers or their pens. He is always dependent upon the freedom and the listening ability of the person in whom he chooses to incarnate Himself, or translate Himself into humanly recognizable shapes or terms. In other words he needs artists and saints to paint the icons of His presence and reveal His face.

On Easter Sunday 1999 Pope John-Paul II wrote a letter to the artists of the world[62] which deserves some attention. Waiving one's initial embarrassment at a letter addressed to a group of people who, for the most part, would have no interest whatever in reading it, or who might see it as provocation or even as a joke, and making allowances for some presumptuous presuppositions, condescending preambles, and selective readings of history, the content is, for the most part, striking and original.

For someone who has lived in Ireland over the last fifty years it does seem like an obscenity to suggest that there has always been a fruitful dialogue between the Church and artists of every kind for many centuries. However, taking the larger perspective and quoting the Romanesque, Gothic and Renaissance periods to prove your case can prove somewhat more convincing. However, whether there has or whether there hasn't, it is such a dialogue that the Pope wishes to intitiate or to continue by this letter. And, as an introduction and a move in that direction, it is welcome and impressive.

The first and most important point for me is that it seems to have been written by himself. In so many other cases one gets the impression that the text has been written by a committee of canon lawyers, and groomed with a fine comb for any ambiguities or stimulants. The quotes here are so often idiosyncratic, and at times from Polish poets, that it is hard to envisage them coming from Vatican sources. Indeed, it is easier to believe in the continued inspiration of the Pontiff by The Holy Spirit after reading this particular text.

It takes a very personal note and is addressed to 'you, to whom I feel closely linked by experiences reaching far back in time and which have indelibly marked my life'. Such experiences refer, presumably, not just to artists and artistic works which have moved him, but to his own artistic endeavours as poet and dramatist.

The dialogue between art and religion which he hopes to promote by this letter and which he claims to have 'gone on unbroken through two thousand years of history' is not there 'by historical accident' or out of 'practical need' only. In other words, it is not just because someone was needed to do up the Vatican and Michelangelo happened to be handy. No, this dialogue is 'rooted in the very essence of both religious experience and artistic creativity.' The Pope is also a philosopher and one of the purposes of this letter is to articulate that 'essential' connection between art and religion.

He begins with a traditional presentation of the artist as 'image of God the Creator'. In such a perspective God creates the world out of nothing and the artist is 'in some way' associated with this work. Metaphysically speaking, God alone creates and bestows being and the role of the artist is to manifest this being. 'He accomplishes this task above all in shaping the wondrous "material" of his own humanity.' Now, obviously, each one of us has this specific task to do in terms our own humanity, but the Pope makes a distinction between each one of us and the artists, because 'not all are called to be artists in the specific sense of the term'. This specific sense of the term is 'the special vocation of the artist' which realises itself in their work. 'Their work becomes a unique disclosure of their own being, of what they are and of how they are what they are.' The artist is really a craftsman – and the Pope uses the Polish word to show a lexical link between the word 'creator' and the word 'craftsman' – who shapes already existing material into forms that reveal their inner reality and communicate these to other people. In such a perspective, which is essentially the Aristotelian and later Thomistic one of God as all-powerful creator and the world as his product, the emphasis is on causality, power and the huge and unbridgeable chasm between the created and the uncreated world, between the creator and the creature. In such a world, the artist is no more than an obedient servant, a humble craftsman, an unworthy recipient of the gift. This is the world of Being where God is everything and we are nothing.

From section three of his text, however, the Pope makes a considerable paradigmatic shift. He starts quoting Polish poets and he introduces the notion of beauty as another transcendental, or approach to God, which is unique, specific and distinct from the metaphysics of causality.

> The theme of *beauty* is decisive for a discourse on art. ...The link between *good* and *beautiful* stirs fruitful reflection. In a certain sense, beauty is the *visible form* of the good, just as the good is *the metaphysical condition of beauty*. This was well understood by the Greeks who, by fusing the two concepts, coined a term which embraces both: *kalokagathia*, or *beauty-goodness*. On this point Plato writes: 'The power of the Good has taken refuge in the nature of the Beautiful'.... The artist has a special relationship to beauty. In a very true sense it can be said that beauty is the vocation bestowed on him by the Creator in the gift of 'artistic talent' ...'

This is the kernel and the key. It leaves itself open to several interpretations. The letter is addressed 'to all who are passionately dedicated to the search for new "epiphanies" of beauty.' The word 'epiphany' is in inverted commas and is the key word. Beauty and art become epiphanies of God in our world. That is a very different presentation of the truth of the Incarnation from the one that a metaphysics of causality and power are forced to defend. But, as the Pope has said, quoting Plato, 'the power of the good has taken refuge in the nature of the beautiful.' The power of the good is being, but the nature of the good is love. There are four transcendentals. In other words, there are four really distinct yet equally viable ways to stretch beyond ourselves and to reach God. The way being valorized in this letter, and the way which in the past was somewhat neglected by the Church, is the way of beauty. To present this way, the Pope in section five of his letter, traces the relationship between 'art and the mystery of the Word made flesh.' He does this not by reference to the usual theologians and dogmatic statements. From the Church's tradition he calls on St Francis as our guide and uses the later Franciscan, St Bonaventure's commentary on his founder: 'In things of beauty, he contemplated the One who is supremely beautiful, and, led by the footprints he found in creatures, he followed the Beloved everywhere.' There is, the Pope tells us, 'a corresponding approach in Eastern spirituality.' In other words, he is breathing with what he has called the other lung of the Church, which is an equivalent image to the left brain in contemporary parlance. This would be the lived experience of the presence of God, not as one, all-powerful creator, but as triune, vulnerable lover; not as all-powerful, untouchable, impervious cause, but as self-surrendering, ever-present Spirit. This is a theology of presence rather than of power, of paternity rather than of causality, of interpenetration in love rather than of eternal separation into created and uncreated being. Such a perspective translates itself into a theology of beauty in nature, of music in thought, of poetry in word, of liturgy in worship.

The most basic fact of John Paul II's faith and philosophy is the primal epiphany of 'God who is Mystery' is Jesus Christ. He quotes his own encyclical *Fides et Ratio* to stress that this is 'the central point of reference for an understanding of the enigma of human existence, the created world and God himself.' He reminds us that Judaism, from which Christianity burgeoned, explicitly condemned most forms of art as representation or imagery of the invisible and inexpressible God. But since God came on earth in human form, it has become possible to paint him, to write about him, to depict scenes of his life, to present this reality in plays, films, music, etc. The incarnation, as well as showing us the way, the truth and the life, has also 'unveiled a new dimension of beauty'. He quotes Paul Claudel and Marc Chagall describing sacred scripture as 'a sort of immense vocabulary' on the one hand and as 'an iconographic atlas' on the other. There is a specific acknowledgement of Byzantine art and in particular the icon as the inspired embodiment of that new dimension of beauty unveiled in the Incarnation. One of the most important and exciting sentences in this letter is that '*the icon is a sacrament*'. These words are emphasized by italics and even though they are attributed to the theology of the East, the Pope elaborates in his own words that 'by analogy with what occurs in the sacraments, the icon makes present the mystery of the Incarnation in one or other of its aspects.'

The letter ends with that crazy but wonderful line of Dostoyevsky which the Pope hails as a 'profound insight': 'beauty will save the world'. And he continues: 'Beauty is a key to the mystery and a call to transcendence. It is an invitation to savour life and to dream of the future.'

Another inspirational part of this text concerns the role of the Holy Spirit in both God and the world in general, and in the realm of art in particular. The Holy Spirit, the Breath (ruah) has been present from the beginning, before Jesus Christ came on earth. The Holy Spirit blows where it will. Then comes a poetic outburst, so unusual in papal letters: 'What affinity, he says, between the words "breath – breathing" and "inspiration"! The Spirit is the mysterious Artist of the universe.' Again this is a most suggestive and inspiring antiphon, but its precise meaning is ambiguous. The Pope quotes the beautiful passage from Genesis where 'the earth was without form and void, and darkness was on the face of the deep; and the Spirit of God was moving over the face of the waters.' And later he gives a much more daring and contemporary quotation from Adam Mickiewicz, a Polish poet writing 'at a time of great hardship for his Polish homeland': 'From chaos there rises the world of the spirit'. It is almost as if he is saying that in a time of seeming chaos both in the Church and in the world, there is space for the Spirit to move and that this movement becomes articulate and receives form through the ministry of the artist. Because the Pope holds that not only does the Spirit work through chosen artists who believe, but 'every genuine inspiration contains some tremor of that "breath" with which the Creator Spirit suffused the work of creation from the very beginning.' This means that 'even in situations where culture and the Church are far apart, art remains a kind of bridge to religious experience.'

Not only are art works kinds of sacraments, but artists have a specific priesthood. The Pope quotes the Constitution on Sacred Liturgy from Vatican II which 'did not hesitate to consider artists as having "a noble ministry" and he quotes Dante approvingly when the latter refers to his own *Divine Comedy* as 'the sacred poem,/ to which both heaven and earth have turned their hand.' Through the work of artists, we are told in *Gaudium et Spes,* 62,: 'the knowledge of God can be better revealed and the preaching of the Gospel can become clearer to the human mind.' And finally, he quotes by name the Dominican theologian, Marie Dominique Chenu, who was silenced in the 1950s for his teachings on these points, but rehabilitated in time to become one of the major influences at the Second Vatican Council. His was the notion of 'the signs of the times' which we are encouraged to read as manifestations or epiphanies of the Holy Spirit, not just in apostolic times but in our contemporary world. The quotation here given by the Pope is highly significant. Chenu says that historians of theology must give due attention in their studies to works of art, both literary and figurative, which in their own way are 'not only aesthetic representations, but genuine "sources" of theology'. This is very strong speaking. How could a work of art become a 'source' of theology if it were not a direct inspiration of the Holy Spirit as the Scriptures have been recognised to be?

From the other side of the spectrum, Seamus Heaney has been outlining, somewhat tentatively, how such a dialogue might work. He gives an image in poem viii from 'Squarings' in his collection *Seeing Things* :

The annals say: when the monks of Clonmacnoise
Were all at prayers inside the oratory
A ship appeared above them in the air.

The anchor dragged along behind so deep
It hooked itself into the altar rails
And then, as the big hull rocked to a standstill,

A crewman shinned and grappled down the rope
And struggled to release it. But in vain.
'This man can't bear our life here and will drown,'

The abbot said, 'unless we help him.' So
They did, the freed ship sailed, and the man climbed back
Out of the marvellous as he had known it.

Heaney used the occasion of his reception of the Nobel Prize for Literature in 1995 to spell out the role that poetry should be playing in a correctly ordered world. He quoted this poem as the icon of this.

Poetry is an 'order'. The assembly in Stockholm provided an occasion and a ceremony for 'Crediting Poetry'. The Nobel Prize acts as a kind of 'space-station' which allows the poet to take a 'space-walk' as if he were in a space-ship. Poetry is 'both the ship and the anchor', Heaney continues, and the place it is carrying us to is 'the "temple inside our hearing" which the passage of the poem calls into being.' Poetry is 'the unappeasable pursuit of this note.' Just as in *The Gigli Concert*, poetry is training you to 'sing yourself to where the singing comes from.' And that place is the altar 'where he expends himself in shape and music'. And the note he sounds is identified and authenticated 'as a ring of truth within the medium itself.'[63]

And, as in the Gospel story of the healed and freed who were told to go and show themselves to the priests, not just to get official confirmation but to show what healing and freedom meant, so the crewman needs to be helped by the monks 'out of the marvellous as he had known it.' Because poetry cannot remain there. What the 'necessary' poetry must always do is 'touch the base of our sympathetic nature' in a way that is 'true to the impact of external reality' while remaining 'sensitive to the inner laws of the poet's being.' Such poetic form as well as being both the ship and the anchor is also 'a buoyancy and a holding' which can achieve 'the birth of the future we desire'. And that future is neither a foregone conclusion nor a predestined plan. It is the future we desire and that is precisely why we need poets to decipher it.

This is the specific 'ministry' of the poet which, as Heaney says, is credited with an authority of its own. 'The poet is credited with a power to open unexpected and unedited communications between our nature and the nature of the reality we inhabit.' This is the aspect of poetry which is essential for spiritual exploration by any person in whatever country or century. It is what allows originality to be tapped, the personal to be touched, the unprecedented to be tolerated. It is 'the idea of imagination as a shaping spirit which it is wrong to disobey.'[64] There are some religious people who would see the play of imagination and the obedience to impulse as 'at best luxury or licentiousness, at worst heresy or treason'. But this is not so. There is a genuine 'inspiration' upon which depends 'the survival of the valid self.' Obedience to such a 'stereometric' impulse finds its validation in 'the jurisdiction of achieved form'. The work of art is an icon of the Spirit when it represents the obedient submission to such prompting. We cannot integrate, assume, transfigure, save, humanity by denying, suppressing, eradicating what is essentially part of it. Heaney describes poetry in Mandelstam's image as 'a dancing chemical formula which integrates reactions perceptible to the ear.'[65] There must be room, in any comprehensive account of human life, for the imaginative leap which may transgress the limits to which we have become accustomed, and leads to uncharted territory, 'the figure of a Chinese fugitive escaping by leaping from junk to junk across a river crammed with junks, all moving in opposite directions.' Here we have neither map nor guide, and may be required to sacrifice some of what we had believed to be absolute and sacred. Such poets deny and refute the uncomprehending caricature of themselves by religious authorities as hedonistic and irreligious. Some may be. But the kind of poetry and the kind of poet I am describing here are passionately religious. They also recognize the necessity for organisation, whether of words or of people, the need to have structure, law, reason. But in the Church, they find it impossible to accept the exclusion of one of the basic principles that makes us human, that 'epitome of chemical suddenness' which is the movement of originality, in the fullest sense of the word, and the source of poetic utterance.

The poet is 'a lyric woodcutter singing in the dark wood of the larynx' the song of humanity which refuses to abandon or deny its essential reality. Reason and 'the golden sun of geometry' are not enough. Christianity must mean the discernment that allows us to follow both the path opened to us by Christ, and the red thread of our own idiosyncratic, personal life's journey. Anything less is Monothelite heresy.

# CHAPTER TWELVE

# BAITING THE BULL

The eighties and nineties were a time for exploring the darker side. A number of courageous and dexterous matadors approached the bull and lunged at its most sensitive areas. Playwright Tom Murphy had been showing us the unromantic shadow side since 1961, when *A Whistle in the Dark,* presented in Dublin and later in London, introduced us to 'the most anthropoidal family of the year'. As one English critic wrote: 'The only thing that separates his characters from a bunch of wild gorillas is their ability to speak with an Irish accent. The play will probably set back Ireland's reputation for civilisation at least 100 years.' So Lady Bracknell was alive and well in London deploring the lack of civilisation and respectability in this Irish writer. The theatre in the second half of the century was busily deconstructing the romantic clichés of the first half: Mother Ireland, the Rose of Tralee, Cathleen ni Houlihan; innocent colleens and virginal maidens on the one hand, fighting men, noble patriots and Aran islanders, strong silent extras for *Finian's Rainbow* or *The Wizard of Oz,* on the other. Joxer Daly, Fluther Good and The Borstal Boy did much to shatter such illusions. But they were nothing compared with the acts to follow.

Half the problem with allowing the 'other voice' to sound is getting rid of archetypes that represent our own hatred of ourselves. Every country and every culture has its own scape-goat hatreds. For Catholic-Gaelic Ireland the most obvious hate-figures are Oliver

Cromwell and Judas Iscariot. They are embedded in every Irish psyche as the ultimate oppressors and traitors. Each one received the full extent of all Brendan Kennelly's experience, versatility, craftsmanship and power in 1983 and 1991 respectively. His obsession with otherness, with introducing himself and ourselves to the 'enemy' we have to learn how to love, finds its most demanding and appropriate protagonists in the archetypal enemy and the icon of apostasy in the Roman Catholic Irish psyche:

> I don't think any Irishman is complete as an Irishman until he becomes an Englishman, imaginatively speaking. I was reared to hate and fear Cromwell, the legends, the folklore of my own parish, the unquestioning hatred of him, which was then transferred to England. That appalled me when I began to try to think ... Cromwell is an ordinary experiment in my own psyche: that I am giving voice to a man who made trees wither. The worst thing you can say in the part of the country I grew up in is 'the curse of Cromwell on you' and I wanted to turn that curse into a blessing.[66]

As always, Kennelly describes the success of his venture in a story:

> I got a punch in the jaw one night crossing O'Connell Bridge from a man who said 'Aren't you the bastard that had a good word for him! Aren't you the fellow that's making a hero out of him?' ... And I said, 'No, he's a man, you're a man, I'm a man'. And he said: 'Drogheda!' He had all the clichés ... All of us are victims of clichés we don't even begin to suspect.

With Cromwell behind him and after eight years of 'clearing a space' within himself, he lets us hear the voice of Judas. This sounds forth in a 378-page epic. We have to marvel at the almost unlimited capacity of this poet to act as ventriloquist and I use the word in its original Latin sense of 'speaking from the belly', to evacuate such inner spaces:[67]

and clear a space for himself
Like Dublin city on a Sunday morning
About six o'clock
Dublin and myself are rid of our traffic then
And I am walking.

This further task of unearthing the aboriginal traitor was evisceration of the most penetrating kind. We must be grateful and aghast at the capacity of this poet to haul these monsters out of our depths:

To have been used so much, and without mercy
And still be capable of rediscovering
In itself the old nakedness.

Satan is an even more difficult scapegoat to rehabilitate. In 1983 Tom Murphy dramatised the new Ireland of prosperous business tycoons and middle-class suburban affluence and ennui. In *The Gigli Concert*, a depressed Irish property developer, Man, as he is called throughout the play, has five manic 'consultations' with an English dynamatologist. The Irishman is the archetypal Irish business success of the sixties, a builder and property developer. He could be Harry from *A Whistle in the Dark* twenty years on. A self-made man, he has spent most of his time and energy getting his two million into the bank. But now he is dissatisfied. He has a wife and child but the would-be bliss of domesticity frustrates him to violence and obscenity. He wants something more than this. He articulates his desire as wanting to sing like the Italian tenor Beniamino Gigli. He has selected Mr J. P. W. King to help him make that happen. Mr King is English. 'Very cold people the English, the British.' 'Sorry about that, old boy, but would we now choose to be superior if we could help it?' The English half of the equation is a Mr King whose empire is 'located somewhere now in – what's them little islands called?' J. P. W. represents the success story of Graeco-Roman education, a dessicated skeleton with an overused brain. Man, who is the bit that was left behind in all that enlightened education 'could always size a man up more from the sound he makes than from what he's saying.' He is trying to find within himself that original pure note that he hears when Gigli sings. He is Adam remembering an original moment in the garden of paradise when the original sin against his nature (exemplified by the specimen dynamatologist standing before him) happened. 'No, it was not a deed. Adam did not lose his head ... he gained a head.... He started thinking and consciousness – thinking – and self-consciousness crept in, which is existential guilt, which is original sin.' J. P. W. goes on with his exegesis of what happened: 'It was much later that the screwing started. Mind-numbing stuff to stop those very feelings of simultaneous innocence and guilt'. Then they went on to 'clearing the jungle, developing it, mind-numbing drudgery to stop the pain – what had they lost, what was the beauty they were longing for? On to milking the goats, cutting the grass, trying to get Cain to toe a more conservative and respectable line, standardised activity, routine trivia, looking for the new security ... And all the time trying to obliterate that side of their nature that was innocent and beautiful, as if it was the side that was vulgar, vicious, mean, ruthless, offensive, dangerous, obscene. Benimillo, what are you doing? ... Benimillo!' And Man, as Adam has gone to the record player to hear the original sound of his own purity: Gigli singing 'Dai Campi, Dai Prati'. During the singing and the listening, 'man's' attitude softens, the stage directions tell us, 'and a few whimper-like sounds escape.' It is Man, as Irish person, *a la recherche du temps perdu*.

Fintan O'Toole, using a quotation from Jung, has an interesting reading of the play:

> If salvation and damnation are thus identified with each other, as two parts of the one whole, then the approach to the Faust story which we might expect from Murphy cannot be the traditional one ... Jung does with the protagonists of Faust, Faust himself and Mephistopheles, the devil who is his familiar and tempter, what Murphy does with salvation and

damnation, making them not separate entities, but two parts of the one whole: 'Faust, the inept, purblind philosopher, encounters the dark side of his being, his sinister shadow, Mephistopheles, who in spite of his negating disposition, represents the true spirit of life as against the arid scholar who hovers on the brink of suicide.' Substitute J. P. W. King for Faust and the Irishman for Mephistopheles in this interpretation of the myth, and you have a precise description of what happens in the course of *The Gigli Concert*.[68]

The play moves through the meeting of these two halves of the person towards a moment where the impossible is made possible on stage and one of them does sing as Gigli. Song is existence, as Rilke says, and this is the level of being that Murphy is trying to reach in us through the drama. And it is a dramatic moment, one that could not be activated through any other artistic medium. The play is the thing. Before this moment J. P. W. King addresses the audience: 'You are going to ask me what is magic. In a nutshell … new mind over old matter.' Later he tells them that 'the soul of the singer is the subconscious self.' But getting to that point and actually singing in that way requires that you 'wait, wait, wait … and wait … until the silence is pregnant with the tone urgent to be born.' Then with the 'Abyss sighted' … Leeeep! (Leap) Pluh-unnge! (Plunge) … (Sigh of relief) Aaah! Rebirth of ideals, return of self-esteem, future known.' This is the moment where the stage instructions tell us: 'He cues in his imaginary orchestra and we get the orchestral introduction to 'Tu Che A Dio Spiegasti L'Ali', and he sings the aria to its conclusion (Gigli's voice): triumphant, emotional ending.' After which he cries out: 'Mama! Mama! Don't leave me in this dark.' The last lines of the play are: 'Do not mind the pig-sty, Benimillo … mankind still has a delicate ear … that's it … that's it … sing on forever … that's it.' The play is an act, a deed, a song, which reawakens an original moment. It tries to follow the singing back to the source. This moment is capturing what Heidegger says of Rilke's poetry, that it is a kind of song which opens up the possibility of being in a way that is more real than our everyday existence in the workaday world. Most of us are commercial travellers through life, looking for what's on offer, with an eye to the best bargain. We have a covetous vision of things. We are calculating. We are working things out in our heads. Song moves us from head work to heart work, it accomplishes existence in us. Not any kind of song but 'a song whose sound does not cling to something that is eventually attained, but which has already shattered itself even in the sounding, so that there may occur only that which was sung itself.'[69] Such singing is neither seduction nor business. It is not purposeful. It is beyond all that. It is back to what we are. Rilke has perhaps come nearest to singing it in words:[70]

Song, as you have taught it, is not desire,
not wooing any grace that can be achieved;
song is reality. Simple, for a god.
But when can we be real? When does he pour

the earth, the stars, into us? Young man,
it is not your loving, even if your mouth
was forced wide open by your own voice - learn

to forget that passionate music. It will end.
True singing is a different breath, about
nothing. A gust inside the god. A wind.

Our culture has been built on a lie and Christianity has helped to promote and sustain that lie. And the lie is this: that it is possible to work out in our heads a logical system which will give us access to ultimate truth, to being. The name of such a system is philosophy and the particular branch of that 'science' that deals with 'being' and places it within our intellectual grasp is 'metaphysics'. Christianity borrowed that system, refined it and inserted into it the geometry of the God who had been revealed in Jesus Christ. Those who were very gifted intellectually, and who had the time, could master this intricate system and could become masters of metaphysics. They could teach some very gifted disciples. The rest would acknowledge that the mystery was too deep for them, would be thankful that there were masters who actually did understand the meaning of such intricate designs, would humbly accept the *Reader's Digest* version, or learn off the precis from a penny catechism, or chew on jawbreaking terminology to anaesthetise their curiosity.

Throughout this century the artists of the world have been trying to tell us that metaphysics is less like mathematics and more like music. Being is not business. Reality is something we touch rather than something we grasp. Song is existence, it wells up through us from the depths.

The only real contact with being, the only language left to sing it, is poetry of a certain kind. Not just any poetry. There are good poets and bad poets, there is poetry for decoration or for propaganda, there is poetry for those in love and for those in mourning. But there is also a metaphysical poetry: poetry that takes it upon itself to give utterance to being. ('And a few whimper-like sounds escape'.)

Each of us from earliest childhood is aware of 'being', not as a something in the world, but as a well-spring in the back of our minds, like the air we breathe. Metaphysical poetry opens our eyes to what we have already always known. It makes us aware of what we have never really adverted to. It is a revelation of being, an epiphany. It shows us the everyday world suffused by the light of being which always remains invisible and yet energises everything.

Great poets dwell in the secret places of the earth and their essential heartwork is to produce honey from these rocks. They are the bees of the invisible, as Rilke says. Their poetry is language drenched in the moisture of being. The object of metaphysics is never present, it is not there. It is a no-thing. And yet when the poet describes the things around us, the words say more than the thing, and that 'more' is the breath of being. The poet who says more is the one who dwells in that place within, which is in contact with this reality, and so allows the breath of being to be caught on the sprockets of each word, and thus secrete itself into our culture as a luminosity which coats the poem as it emerges with its phosphorescence.

So there is no guaranteed formula for production. The process of 'doing' metaphysics – which is the 'doing' of poetry – is one which at all times must reinvent 'being' anew. It is like 'making' love. It doesn't happen without the added extra, the unknown quantity. But this is what happens with every experience of life, in life. It is always an unconscious and secret experience at another level. There is a delicate shimmering gossamer around every reality, which we, in our hasty agendas and business schedules, invariably overlook or ignore. This reticent subtext to experience is what poetry helps us to illuminate. It is almost as if we have to go back into the darkroom of our experience and develop these implications from the negatives of the day-to-day photo call. Because this second level transcends the normal day-to-day experience, we have to invent butterfly nets to entrap the fragrance or filter the fine dust that issues from every contact with reality, but which gets dispersed in the normal process of harvesting what we usually feed ourselves on. It is never the content of what we glean from this harvest, nor is it ever the ideas contained in our heads that give access to 'being'. No, it is the contact, the meeting, the impact of reality which creates the sparks that we need to recover if we are to have any inkling of the real meaning, the metaphysical weight of these same experiences. This is what essential poetry tries to achieve.

In an interview in 1970 Brian Friel is quoted as saying:

> I would like to write a play that would capture the peculiar spiritual, and indeed material, flux that this country is in at the moment. This has got to be done, for me anyway, at a local level, and hopefully this will have meaning for other people in other countries. The canvas can be as small as you wish, but the more accurately you write and the more truthful you are the more validity your play will have for the world.'[71]

In 1994 he staged the play which does precisely that for the situation I am trying to describe here. *Molly Sweeney* is a parable about Ireland. The name combines various memories and has a faintly mocking tone. Molly is used as a name in many popular songs like Molly Malone and My Irish Molly, but it received a more suspect connotation in Molly Bloom of Joyce's *Ulysses*. Sweeney on the other hand has both literary and mythological references. In 1985 Seamus Heaney had published *Sweeney Astray*, which was his translation of the *Buile Suibhne*. This is a story in Irish, dating from the seventeenth century, but with origins in the seventh century, about an Irish King, Sweeney, who is outraged that the priest, Ronan, is building a church in his territory. He confronts Ronan and throws his psalter in a lake. An otter returns the book to Ronan, who curses Sweeney. Sweeney is thereupon changed into a bird-man, with a bird-brain, living in the trees. He is mad, but it is the madness of a poet. He composes prophetic poems.

There are only three characters in Friel's play, who sit on stage like three 'charges' in an heraldic shield. Molly is centre stage and beside her are Frank, her husband, and Mr Rice, an eye specialist. Molly is blind and her husband wants her to have an operation, which Mr Rice is eager to perform. An important fourth character who does not appear in person is Molly's father. He was a judge during the early years of the Free State. He now lives with Molly in a walled garden. He teaches her the names of the flowers. They live in a self-contained universe. Her work is massage therapy. She has a world of touch in which she is able to mould her own relationships. Swimming is her hobby which allows her to move 'rhythmically through that enfolding world.' Molly is essentially content at the beginning of the play, describing herself as 'disadvantaged not deprived.' She only agrees to the operation on her eyes because of her husband's expectations and the doctor's insistence. Her husband Frank is a credulous sucker for every novelty. He moves from Iranian goats, which are a disaster in the Irish climate, to bees and finally moves off altogether to Abyssinia. He is a dilettante. This operation is one of the many causes he embraces without discernment or foresight. He represents the twentieth-century entrepreneurial spoliator, the quick-buck innovator who moves in to get the 'hello money' and moves out when the plant won't take root. He is the kind of charlatan that Ireland is presently prey to. 'We are no longer West Britons, we are East Americans', Friel has warned, and we are hardly capable of assessing all the exotic flotsam and jetsam that washes onto our shores.

The other protagonist, Mr Rice, is a failed specialist who drinks too much and never really made it. Molly is his last chance to work a miracle. So, Molly's blindness, with which she is perfectly happy, is being sacrificed for the kind of 'vision' on offer from the two inadequates who surround her. She is being persuaded to buy into an advertised world that doesn't measure up to its promises. At the geo-political level it is almost like Ireland's entry into Europe as a member of the European Community. We were told we would hit the jackpot, that we would be mollycoddled by our munificent neighbours into a world without want or worry. Once the operation has been performed and we are inconsolably disappointed, we cease to be 'Miracle Molly' and go back to being Mrs Sweeney as far as the doctor is concerned. 'And what sort of world did you expect, Mrs Sweeney?' Mr Rice asks defensively.

Molly ends up neither seeing nor being blind. She is in an in-between state where she can no longer remain at home but has to live out her days in an institution, getting rare visits from friends and rarer ones from her husband. 'Blindsight' is the important term for this limbo. Blindsight is a physiological condition. The cortex prevents what is actually perceived from reaching consciousness. To avoid an accident from an oncoming car, for instance, you react not because you see the car coming towards you but because of some other instinctual part of the cortex moving you out of the way. So, the paradox of so-called 'progress' is presented dramatically: were we better off in the 50s in a smothering self-contained garden, which could boast almost zero per cent criminality, or have we gained a certain freedom and welfare?

Many of us would say no. These would claim that we were mad

to leave that insulated security. The same lobby might also hold that most of these so-called artists who pretend to be offering us some new kind of vision are insane. Insanity has always been one of the dangers that artists and others who courageously oppose the sanity of the majority have had to face, either as an accusation or a very real possibility – either as a cause of their 'vision' or as a result of its dismissal by the majority of their contemporaries. Molly Sweeney is certainly portrayed as a victim of untrustworthy visionaries. Hers is a cautionary tale.

# CHAPTER THIRTEEN

# GENTLING THE BULL

In *The Brothers Karamazov*, Dostoyevsky offers a terrifying picture of the Minotaur in the person of the Grand Inquisitor, who is meant to depict the Catholic Church at its most totalitarian and ferocious. Christ returns to earth and is confronted by this authoritarian figure. The aim of the inquisitor is to send Christ back where he came from as speedily as possible. Why? Because he incarnated in both his person and his teaching dangerous revolutionary impulses that promised a freedom 'which human beings in their simplicity and innate lawlessness cannot even comprehend, which they fear and dread – for nothing has ever been more unendurable to human society than freedom!' The inquisitor taunts the powerless saviour who has returned on a visit and has renounced his omnipotence: 'You wanted their free love so that they would follow you freely, fascinated and captivated by you. Instead of the strict ancient law, they had in future to decide for themselves with a free heart what was good and what was evil, having only your image before them for guidance.' So, the inquisitor continues, we have corrected your great work. They weren't up to that challenge. It was beyond them, too much for them. So, we felt sorry for them and took over. We, who have a much more realistic and compassionate understanding of humanity, have taken that freedom away from them and replaced it with an authoritarian rule that governs their lives in every detail and removes the worry about how to achieve salvation, how to become free.

The people have become so obedient to the inquisitor that one command from him will turn the mob against this human person of Christ and all will see it as a religious act to have him burnt publicly. 'When the Inquisitor finished speaking, he waited for some time for the Prisoner's reply. His silence distressed him. He saw that the Prisoner had been listening intently to him all the time, looking gently into his face and evidently not wishing to say anything in reply. The old man would have liked him to say something, however bitter and terrible. But he suddenly approached the old man and kissed him gently on his bloodless, aged lips. That was all his answer. The old man gave a start. There was an imperceptible movement at the corners of his mouth; he went to the door, opened it and said to him: "Go, and come no more – don't come at all – never, never!" And he let him out into 'the dark streets and lanes of the city. The Prisoner went away. And the old man? "The kiss glows in his heart, but the old man sticks to his idea."'[72]

A kiss is a way of connecting people in the most intimate exchange, without their necessarily knowing and understanding one another. It is being in touch. It is the language of equals. It allows you to feel the confirmation, the energy, the approval of the person kissing. It is a specific and emotionally charged presence which does not require an overall grasp of the situation, nor does it involve great preparation or skill. In this context it describes a relationship which is neither following an idea nor adopting a technique, it is groping towards someone in the dark. It is heartwork.

John of the Cross and Meister Eckhart use it as an image for what happens in contemplation when we get in touch with God. John, whose spiritual canticles are poems about such encounters, is clear that such a journey involves the dark night of the soul. This necessarily entails going into the dark and exploring the territory of the unconscious until we reach that outer wall of ourselves from which it is possible to touch what is beyond. Once we have befriended this darkness, we come directly into contact with God and we kiss. Commenting on stanza fifteen of his *Spiritual Canticle*, he tells us that 'this kiss is the union in which the soul is made equal with God through love.' This is the equality of lovers. It is the equality achieved by humility, by that descent into the ground of our being until we reach the vanishing point – what Solzhenitsyn calls *The First Circle* of ourselves – where we are nothing, and where every zero equals zero. At this place, this zone, which Tarkovsky maps out in his film *Stalker*, we are able to meet on the innermost lip of our cultural cocoon anyone else who cares to reach this particular membrane of their own. At this level we are all equal, not because we are the same but because we are unique, the only one of our kind. God, at this point of self-emptying kenosis, becomes one of us – infinities of unique particularity, once-off originals, singular selfhoods. It is interesting to note that when it was feared that the works of John of the Cross might be condemned by the Inquisition, this was one of the passages that was changed.

Analagously, this is the kind of connection we need to make between the conscious part of ourselves and the unconscious. Kissing the dark means caring for it, reaching towards it, welcoming it, reassuring it, taming it. It means befriending the Minotaur.

'Gentling the Bull' is a Zen training process[73] which allows you to get in touch with that aspect of yourself. This involves searching for, finding, catching, taming and riding back home, the bull that is part of everyone's being. It is usually accomplished by meditating on the Bull Pictures, a series of ten paintings by the fifteenth-century Japanese Zen monk Shubun. Traditionally these pictures are attributed to a twelfth-century Zen master. They are kept in Shokoku-ji monastery in Kyoto, where Shubun was a monk. His pictures are said to be copies of the series by Kakuan, which no longer exists. Such traditional Zen training is about becoming truly human. The bull is the wild aspect of the heart. Who has never experienced an uprush of bull-energy, the Japanese ask? Who has never been carried away by the bull? To think of this bull as an enemy is the greatest mistake we can make. The exercises, with the paintings and the poems, try to establish in each of us the correct attitude to the bull. Search for what?, the Zen masters say, the bull has never been missing. But without knowing it, the herdsman estranged himself from himself and so the bull became lost in the dust. Which means that although forgotten the bull does not have to be acquired. It has always been there, and can be re-discovered by suitable exercises or practices. These are specified by the Buddha and derive from his own experience.

We have to undertake some similar exercise or exercises in Europe to start befriending the Minotaur. This will involve both aspects of this reality: the bull-energy within ourselves and the bull-headed xenophobe that is each one of us as part of the mob, the moral majority.

That Brendan Smyth, the first priest in our society to have been publicly exposed as a paedophile and child molester, was subject to the kind of torture he endured in prison, where he was constantly beaten over the head with socks bulging with billiard balls by other prisoners who regarded his crimes as beneath contempt, and qualitatively different from their own; that he had to be buried at midnight and a cement covering put over his grave in case the mob might dig it up to desecrate it; such aspects of the bull say more about our society than they do about the person they are supposed to discredit or denounce. They are signs of a society creating scapegoat monsters and operatic villains which only serve to distance us from the real nature of our own situation and prevent us from identifying the conniving partner and blood relation in our society who is the darker side of ourselves.

In our role as Minotaur we are actually eating ourselves up at the centre of our own labyrinth. We blame the paparazzi, for instance, for hounding their victims and shooting at them indiscriminately and inappropriately. But they are earning their living by providing us with what they know we want, food for the hungry Minotaur inside.

Ted Hughes, the recently deceased British Poet Laureate – himself a victim of the Minotaur for most of his life – in his *Tales of Ovid* (powerful translations of *The Metamorphoses*), describes the fate of Actaeon who, out hunting with his hounds, happens to stumble upon the Goddess Diana bathing naked in a pool. For his foolhardiness she transforms him into a stag. His poem opens:

Destiny, not guilt, was enough
For Actaeon. It is no crime
To lose your way in a dark wood.

His door into the dark, however, changed him into prey. The hunter
became the hunted, as has happened so many who undertook this
journey. 'But then as he circled, his own hounds found him.' He
knew them all by name but:

Where Actaeon had so often strained
Every hound to catch and kill the quarry,
Now he strained to shake the same hounds off –

His own hounds. He tried to cry out:
'I am Actaeon – remember your master,'
But his tongue lolled wordless, while the air

Belaboured his ears with hounds' voices.
Now the hills he had played on so happily
Toyed with the echoes of his death-noises.
His head and antlers reared from the heaving pile.

And swayed – like the signalling arm
Of somebody drowning in surf.
But his friends, who had followed the pack

To this unexpected kill,
Urged them to finish their work. Meanwhile they shouted
For Actaeon – over and over for Actaeon
To hurry and witness this last kill of the day –
And such a magnificent beast –
As if he were absent. He heard his name

And wished he were as far off as they thought him.
He wished he was among them
Not suffering this death but observing

The terrible method
Of his murderers, as they knotted
Muscles and ferocity to dismember

Their own master.
Only when Actaeon's life
Had been torn from his bones, to the last mouthful,

Only then
Did the remorseless anger of Diana,
Goddess of the arrow, find peace.[74]

It is ironic that this poem was published in the year that Diana Spencer, Princess of Wales, was sacrificed to the Minotaur. Her brother used the same imagery as Ted Hughes in Westminster Abbey at her funeral: The Goddess of hunting, Diana, who was hounded to her death. But it is the symptomatic image of ourselves as we goad on the media as Minotaur to devour those parts of ourselves that step out of line.

There are those who no longer believe in any God or any religion because of disappointment with the Churches or because of disillusionment caused by the scandalous and criminal behaviour being daily reported among so-called professional representatives of the clergy and the religious orders. Nothing of the sort should allow us to be deflected from our own particular journey, our own personal connection with the living God. Indeed, such revelations are a healthy clearing of the Augean stables. And the manure being spread by such puncturing of the cess-pool, which is long overdue, can only contribute to more healthy and abundant growth when the springtime comes.

Because the truth is still present, the reality is still alive: God so loved the world that he sent his Son to live with us and to show us how to live in the fullest way possible. Dostoyevsky wrote these words a hundred years ago, three months before his death:

> Fathers and teachers, what is a monk? Among the educated this word is nowadays uttered with derision by some people, and some even use it as a term of abuse. And it is getting worse as time goes on. It is true, alas, it is true that there are many parasites, gluttons, abusers and arrogant hypocrites among the monks. Educated people would point this out: 'You are idlers and useless members of society,' they say, 'you live on the labour of others. You are shameless beggars.' And yet think of the many meek and humble monks there are, monks who long for solitude and fervent prayer in peace and quiet. These attract less their attention, and how surprised they would be if I told them that the salvation of Russia would perhaps once more come from the monks … In their solitude they keep the image of Christ pure and undefiled for the time being, in the purity of God's truth, which they received from the fathers of old, the apostles and martyrs, and when the time comes they will reveal it to the wavering righteousness of the world. That is a great thought. The star will shine forth from the east.
>
> That is what I think of the monk, and is it false, is it arrogant? Look at the worldly and all those who set themselves up above God's people on earth, has not God's image and God's truth been distorted in them? They have science, but in science there is nothing but what is subject to the senses. The spiritual world, the higher half of man's being, is utterly rejected, dismissed with a sort of triumph, even with hatred. The world has proclaimed freedom, especially in recent times, but what do we see in this freedom of theirs? Nothing but slavery and self-destruction.
>
> The monastic way is different. People even laugh at obedience, fasting and prayer, and yet it is through them that the way lies to real, true freedom: I cut off all superfluous and

unnecessary needs, I subdue my proud and ambitious will, and with God's help I attain freedom of the spirit and with it spiritual joy!

Which of them is more capable of conceiving a great idea and serving it – the rich in their isolation or those freed from the tyranny of habit and material things? The monks are reproached for their solitude but it is the rich not the monks who live in isolation.

In the olden days, leaders came from our midst, why cannot it happen again now? The salvation of Russia comes from the people ... Therefore, take care of the people, and educate them quietly. That is your great task as monks, for this people is a Godbearer.[75]

For the people of Ireland, the greatest tragedy of the approaching millennium would be the loss of their deep connection with God, their belief in Christianity, their religious sensibility.

All these can and should be maintained through the dialogue that must happen between artists and the Church. Artists must follow the anchor hooked into the altar rails. Much has to change, many anachronisms need to be discarded, many superstitions purified, many fears allayed. We are a different, more affluent, better-educated population than ever before. We need a relationship with God and an understanding of Christianity that corresponds to and connects with the reality of who we are. Artists have always claimed to be in touch with the people; their art found its source in this reality, which was often the reason why it was condemned in the past. The dialogue between who we are and who Christ is will lead us all to a fuller and more comprehensive way of being. Louis MacNeice suggests its tentativeness in his poem 'Coda':

But what is that clinking in the darkness?
Maybe we shall know each other better
When the tunnels meet beneath the mountain.

In the meantime, it would be wise for us not to throw out everything we have known and have been in the past, in a fit of despair or disillusionment or even a desire to be rid of so much junk. Let another poet lead us in less extravagant and more accurate procedures:[76]

### Votive Lamp

The pope and the sacred heart
went off on the back of a cart,
and I've tried to find a home
for the child of Prague.

If that lamp weren't the exact
shape of a brandy glass there might be some chance
that I'd part with it.

Small chance, though.

If I'd been brought up in the clear light of reason,
I might feel differently.

But I often come home in the dark

and, from the hall door,

in the red glow
I can discern
a child's violin
and, coming closer,
a plover;
the photograph of a dead friend;
three hazelnuts gathered from a well;
and three leather-skinned shamans
who flew all the way from Asia
on one card.

> I designed none of this and don't know whether
> sacred objects and images tend to cluster
> around a constant light,
> or whether,
> the small star's constancy,
> through other lives and other nights
> now confers some sanctity
> on my life's bric-a-brac.

Keeping the image, the icon of Christ, pure and undefiled, is basically remembering His essential nothingness, the *paupertas, nuditas, humilitas Christi,* which we have been covering up ever since it was announced. He emptied himself of his divinity, he poured himself out, so that there would be nothing left to come between us and the hidden reality of the Godhead. Kierkegaard, after St Paul, reminds us: 'Christ is nothing, never forget it Christianity.' He disappeared, went away, left us, blotted himself out, so that we could find the new reality which is the Spirit within ourselves.

But we have insisted on hanging him up as a barrier between ourselves as fellow Christians, and as a rood-screen between ourselves and the God who is.

Christianity has presented Christ as an image, as a model, as a picture of perfection. This is precisely the problem. Christianity turned itself into a pursuit of perfection rather than an achievement of completeness. The cross became an external and impossible point of unnatural oblong striving, rather than an internal even-armed crucial division of ourselves into quadripartite areas and functions of consciousness and unconsciousness, thinking and feeling, sensation and intuition.

The cross is simply the sign of God's insane love. His wounds are proof of his vulnerability – the Latin word for wound. He has a heart, contary to all the rumours spread by the Greeks, and we have access to it, power over it, endless possibilities to break it. This is the scandal, the madness, the folly of the cross. But there is no understanding of this mystery until it breaks out in us as individual people in the way it erupted through the flesh of St Francis of Assisi. Stigma is the exaggerated flowering of the cross of Christ. It is the same love of God overwhelming and bursting through the pores of those who have accepted to respond. Anything else is irrelevant unless it be a marker, a reminder, a re-enactment of the original bloomsday of that love.

But because we are human we continue to represent to ourselves – in iron, in stone, in precious metal, in sculpture, in music, in verse, in liturgy, in drama and in film – this central reality of our lives. Sometimes we do this in execrable taste, sometimes we do it with exquisite artistry. In Ireland the most beautiful high crosses in the world dot the countryside dating from at least the eighth century and probably much earlier. These have a particular and identifiable design. A circle is inserted into the arms of the cross, which experts have explained as imitating jewelry, brooches, etc., or as a way of preventing the heavy arms of the celtic cross from falling off or being damaged. These are tedious explanations and the crosses stand for all to see and for each to invest with their own interpretation.[77]

Jung says that such symbols are universal. In all religions, the circle and the cross are well-known symbols for God. The cross here means the quaternity in all its forms. And these images express the unified wholeness of human beings.

And on the eve of this millennium it is through the foot of this cross that we have to plunge the scalpel, to lance the abcess that centuries of neglect, repression and denial have allowed to fester, so that we can be restored to fullness of health and humanity, and so that His salvation may reach to the ends of the earth.

Thomas Mann, in his attempt to recreate the Faust story, gives us a description of a diving-bell descending into the black depths of the ocean, which is a parable of the task we are setting ourselves to accomplish:

> Adrian spoke of the itch one felt to expose the unexposed, to look at the unlooked-at, the not-to-be and not-expecting-to-be-looked-at. There was a feeling of indiscretion, even of guilt,

bound up with it, not quite allayed by the feeling that science must be allowed to press just as far forwards as it is given the intelligence of scientists to go. The incredible eccentricities, some grisly, some comic, which nature here achieved, forms and features which seemed to have scarcely any connection with the upper world but rather to belong to another planet: these were the product of seclusion, sequestration, of reliance on being wrapped in eternal darkness ... Quite indescribable too was everything that went whisking past the windows in a blur of motion: frantic caricatures of organic life; predatory mouths opening and shutting; obscene jaws, telescope eyes; ... even those that floated passively in the flood, monsters compact of slime, yet with arms to catch their prey, polyps, acalephs, skyphomedusas.'[78]

At every new stage of development, with each manifestation of a more complex form of natural existence, new possibilities for more perfect embodiment of beautiful life occur. But these are not guaranteed. Increase in power, in range, in variety, in complexity, does not automatically ensure emergence as beauty. It sometimes produces the opposite. The gravitational and the beautiful are often in opposition to each other. Beauty is only one tiny possibility among a plethora of potential monstrosities. The history of paleontology in general, as well as in each individual animal, shows embryonic signs of resistance to the more complete and beautiful forms of later evolutionary development. Each new triumph of organic beauty spawned a corresponding gallery of hideous counterparts, beauty always accompanied by the beast. Both are monuments to the original protoplasmic formlessness, the basic nothingness, the shapeless void, which is at the zero-point of all being.

Even though, for us now as human beings, historical development has replaced 'biological' or 'cosmogonic' evolution, which preceded the eventual production of the human species, there are still many aspects of our growth to maturity that mirror our embryological emergence. In other words, even though we will not develop into another kind of species as such, we can still improve what we are, by a corresponding process of selection and struggle. There is always a very subtle connection between what we are and what we could be. Hearing the possible direction of our heartbeat of the present; feeling our way towards the place where a possible escape-route, a breakthough might occur; being sensitive to promptings from the *Zeitgeist*, the Spirit of the times, this is the demanding heartwork of the artist, who sketches improvisations on such possibilities for us to go by and act upon. Art hears, sees, imagines the possibilities that nature resists with all its might. We can see the traces of such stubborn resistance in the redundant leftovers of previous, discarded species. The bellowing Minotaur is the voice of such resistance to the new-look humanity, which art can sense in the pig-sty of the present. 'Mankind still has a delicate ear.' This is not evolution in terms of some external irresistible force relentlessly pursuing its preordained purpose; rather, it is tentative advance through sensitive co-operation between the Spirit of possibility and the ingenuity of the actual. The two great thwarters of any such imaginative advance are paralysing smugness on the one hand and ungrounded ideology on the other.

It is clear that when we explore the dark we will find, as did the travellers in the diving-bell, 'incredible eccentricities', born of repression and sequestration. These are the traces of inner opposition, the obdurate determination to remain as ugly as we are. Each victory for the new and more beautiful leaves behind the embodiment of twisted snarling protest against such progress, such movement towards perfection. When making the comprehensive and complete assessment of the reality that we are, which will also allow for accurate divination of what we might be, we must be prepared for any and every revelation, we must be open and compassionate to all we find. We must also be optimistic and trusting as that imaginative paleontologist, Teilhard de Chardin, advises:

We must try to penetrate our most secret self, and examine our being from all sides ... And so, for the first time in my life perhaps (although I am supposed to meditate every day!), I took the lamp and, leaving the zone of everyday occupations and relationships where everything seems clear, I went down into my inmost self, to the deep abyss whence I feel dimly that my power of action emanates. But as I moved further and further away from the conventional certainties by which social life is superficially illuminated, I became aware that I was losing contact with myself. At each step of the descent a new person was disclosed within me of whose name I was no longer sure, and who no longer obeyed me. And when I had to stop my exploration because the path faded from beneath my steps, I found a bottomless abyss at my feet, and out of it came – arising from I know not where – the current which I dare to call 'my' life.

Stirred by my discovery, I then wanted to return to the light of day and forget the disturbing enigma in the comfortable surroundings of familiar things – to begin living again at the surface without imprudently plumbing the depths of the abyss. But then, beneath this very spectacle of the turmoil of life, there reappeared, before my newly-opened eyes, the unknown that I wanted to escape ... At that moment, as anyone else will find who cares to make the same interior experiment, I felt the distress characteristic to a particle adrift in the universe, the distress which makes human wills founder daily under the crushing number of living things and of stars. And if something saved me, it was hearing the voice of the gospel, guaranteed by divine successes, speaking to me from the depth of the night: *Ego sum, noli timere* (Do not be afraid, I am here).

Yes, O God, I believe it: and I believe it all the more willingly because it is not only a question of my being consoled, but of my being completed.[79]

INTRODUCTION
1. Alexander Solzenitsyn, *The First Circle* (Fontana, 1971), pp. 357-358.

CHAPTER ONE: CLIMBING INTO OUR PROPER DARK
2. Peter Gay, *The Bourgeois Experience, Victoria to Freud,* vol. I: *Education of the Senses* (Oxford, New York, 1984), p. 13.

CHAPTER TWO: MISSHAPPEN GEOMETRIES
3. Saint Cyprian *Treatises, The Fathers of the Church, a New Translation,* (New York, 1958), vol. 36, pp. 125-159. Also *The Divine Office, The Liturgy of the Hours according to the Roman Rite,* vol. III, p. 188 f. and pp. 267*-270*.
4. Charles Davis, *Body as Spirit* (New York, 1976), p. 53.

CHAPTER THREE: RHOMBOIDAL REMOULD
5. Quoted in Maurice Moynihan (ed.) *Speeches and Statements by Eamon de Valera,* 1917-1973 (Dublin, 1980), p. 364.
6. Martin Buber, *Between Man and Man* (New York, 1964), pp. 113-114.
7. Sigmund Freud, *Introductory Lectures on Psychoanalysis,* The Pelican Freud Library (1975), vol I, pp. 370-371.

CHAPTER FOUR: PARALLELOGRAM OF FORCES
8. Anne Baring and Jules Cashford, *The Myth of the Goddess: Evolution of an Image,* pp. 142-143.
9. One of the books that summarizes this theme is *The Chalice and the Blade* by Riane Eisler (New York, 1987).
10. Anthony Stevens, *Archetype: A Natural History of the Self* (London, 1982), p. 181ff. What he says about the topic we are emphasizing is taken for the most part from a study by Corinne Hutt (1972) who concludes that 'creativity, assertiveness and divergent thinking are linked masculine characteristics, and that outstanding abilities in these areas are likely to be manifested early in life... Genetics and neuroendocrinology are the nub of the matter. Physical differences between men and women in height, weight, fat and hair distribution,

body contour, bone structure and muscular development are so obvious that not even the most fanatical behaviourist would attempt to argue that they are other than genetically determined. Moreover, the growth and development of boys and girls are clearly programmed differently from the moment of conception, for the physical superiority of the male begins to manifest itself even in the womb: male foetuses grow faster than females and at birth male infants are both heavier and longer. Thenceforth, from infancy to old age, males have larger and more powerful muscles, their hearts are bigger and stronger, their lungs have greater vital capacity and their basal metabolic rate is higher.'

11. Dudley Young, *Origins of the Sacred* (London: Abacus 1993), pp. 104-112.
12. A. Leroi-Gourhan, *Treasures of Prehistoric Art* (New York, 1967), p. 174.
13. D.W. Winnicott (1896-1971), *The Child, The Family and the Outside World* and *Playing and Reality* (Penguin, 1971).

## CHAPTER SIX: THE FOUR OF THE CROSSROADS + THE SWINGING OF THE DOOR

14. Hugo Rahner, 'The Mystery of the Cross', *Eranos Jahrbuch* 2, pp. 380-387.
15. Rainer Maria Rilke, 'The Young Worksman's Letter', *Rodin and Other Prose Pieces* ( London: Quartet Books, 1986), pp.144-145.

## CHAPTER SEVEN: THE LABYRINTH

16. R. C. Lewontin, 'Genes, Environment and Organisms', *Hidden Histories of Science*, edited by Robert Silvers (London, 1997), p. 136.
17. Oliver Sacks, 'Scotoma: Forgetting and Neglect in Science', in Robert Silvers, op. cit. pp. 177-179. He suggests that the atmosphere in neurology has radically changed and has now 'become very sympathetic to the idea of self-organization, of cerebral and mental organization *emerging* under the influence of experience'.
18. Dermot Keogh, *Twentieth Century Ireland: Nation and State* (Dublin, 1994), p. 29.
19. F. S. L. Lyons, *Culture and Anarchy in Ireland, 1890-1939* (Oxford, 1979), p. 157.

## CHAPTER EIGHT: THE SILKEN THREAD

20. Ottavio Paz, *The Other Voice, Essays on Modern Poetry*, translated by Helen Lane (Harcourt, Brace, Jovanovich, 1991), pp. 150-155.

21. Seamus Heaney, *The Government of the Tongue* (London, 1988), p. 59.

22. George Bernard Shaw, 'The Censorship', *Irish Statesman* II (1928), reprinted in *Banned in Ireland: Censorship and the Irish Writer*, edited by Julia Carlson (Athens: University of Georgia Press, 1990), pp. 133-138.

23. *Selected Joyce Letters*, edited by Richard Ellmann (New York, 1975), p. 129.

24. Rainer Maria Rilke, 'The Young Workman's Letter', (written in February 1922) in *Rodin and Other Prose Pieces* (London 1986), pp. 151-152.

25. 'The Gospel according to Sinéad', interview with Olaf Tyaransen, *Hot Press*, 28 May 1997, p. 21.

26. Frank McCourt, *Angela's Ashes* (London, 1996).

27. Seamus Heaney interviewed by Ian Hargreaves in *Financial Times*, Monday, 10 June 1991.

28. Seamus Heaney, *The Government of the Tongue* (London: Faber&Faber, 1988), p. 96.

29. Richard Pine, *Brian Friel and Ireland's Drama* (London, 1990), p. 17.

30. Ibid, p. 18.


## CHAPTER TEN: ART AND INSANITY

31. C. G. Jung, *Memories, Dreams, Reflections* (Fontana, 1983), pp.146-49.

32. C. G. Jung, 'The Psychogenesis of Mental Diseases', in *The Collected Works*, Bollingen XX (New York, 1960) vol. 3, pp. 170-78.

33. Quotations from letters are taken from *The Complete Letters of Vincent van Gogh*, 2nd ed. (New York Graphic Society, 1978).

34. Anthony Storr, 'The Sanity of True Genius' in *Churchill's Black Dog*, (London, 1989), p. 264.

35. For an accessible presentation of Lacan's abstruse thought on the 'symbolic' father, I found helpful: *Changing Fathers? Fatherhood and Family Life in Modern Ireland*, by Kieran McKeown, Harry Ferguson, Dermot Rooney (Dublin Collins Press, 1998), most especially chapter 2 by Dermot Rooney, pp. 49-77.

36. Franz Kafka, 'Letter to His Father' quoted in 'Kafka's Sense of Identity' Anthony Storr, op. cit., p. 61.

37. Ibid.

38. Ibid., p. 69.
39. George D. Painter, *Marcel Proust* (Penguin, 1983), p. 239.
40. Ibid., p. 585.
41. C. J. Jung, 'Ulysses: a Monologue', in *The Collected Works*, Bollingen XX (New York, 1966), vol. 15, pp. 122-23.
42. Ibid., p. 137, note 3.
43. *Selected Joyce Letters*, edited by Richard Ellman (New York, 1975), p. 692.
44. C. J. Jung, op. cit., vol. 8, p. 513.
45. Ibid., p. 119.
46. Ellmann, op. cit., p. 559.
47. C. J. Jung, op. cit., vol. 8, p. 513.
48. *Finnegans Wake* (Faber, 1975), paperback edition, p. 269.
49. *Finnegans Wake*, p. 18.
50. Ibid., p. 18.
51. Richard Kearney, 'Beckett: The Demythologising Intellect', in *The Irish Mind* (Dublin, 1985), pp. 289-90.
52. Richard Ellmann, *Four Dubliners*, p. 104.
53. Samuel Beckett, *Proust* (New York, 1957), pp. 61-70.
54. Ellmann, op. cit., p. 562.
55. C. G. Jung, op. cit., vol. 8, p. 531.
56. Ibid., pp. 509-511.
57. Ibid., p. 513.
58. Ibid., p. 510.
59. Ibid., p. 511.

CHAPTER ELEVEN: THE POETS AND THE POPE

60. Hans Urs Von Balthasar, *Mysterium Paschale* (Edinburgh, 1990), p. 249.
61. Ibid., pp. 246-247.
62. Letter of His Holiness Pope John Paul II to Artists (Vatican City Press, 1999).
63. Seamus Heaney, *Crediting Poetry, The Nobel Lecture* (Gallery Books), p. 28. Reprinted in *Opened Ground: Poems 1966-1996* (London: Faber&Faber, 1998), p. 466.
64. Seamus Heaney, *Government of the Tongue* (London, 1988), p. 95.
65. Ibid.
66. Interview with Richard Pine, *Irish Literary Supplement*, Spring 1990, p. 22.

67. Brendan Kennelly, *A Time For Voices: Selected Poems 1960-1990* (Bloodaxe Books, 1990), p. 124.
68. Fintan O'Toole, *The Politics of Magic: The Work and Times of Tom Murphy* (Dublin, 1987), p. 167.
69. Martin Heidegger 'What Are Poets For?' in *Poetry, Language, Thought* (Harper & Row, New York, 1971), p. 139.
70. Rainer Maria Rilke, *The Sonnets to Orpheus* (Touchstone, New York, 1985), Part I, 3, p. 23.
71. *The Irish Times*, 12 February 1970.

## CHAPTER THIRTEEN: GENTLING THE BULL

72. Fyodor Dostoyevsky, *The Brothers Karamazov* (Penguin Books, 1969), vol. I, book V, chapter 5, pp. 288-310.
73. Cf. for example *Gentling The Bull, The Ten Bull Pictures, A Spiritual Journey*, comments taken from talks by The Venerable Myokyo-ni, published in association with The Zen Centre, London, 1988.
74. Ted Hughes, *Tales from Ovid*, (London: Faber&Faber, 1997), pp. 105-112. I was introduced to this poem and to a similar reading of it applied to the work of psychoanalysis by John Hughes.
75. Fyodor Dostoyevsky, op. cit. vol. I, book VI, chapter 3, pp. 368-70.
76. Moya Cannon, *Oar*, (Galway: Salmon, 1994) pp. 47-8.
77. Everything I know about high crosses in Ireland comes from conversations with, lectures given, and fieldtrips organized by Peter Harbison. Those who cannot avail of his inimitable and electrifying communication of understanding and enthusiasm in person can find his written account in *The High Crosses of Ireland*, 3 vols. (Bonn, 1992), and, in more popular form, in *Ancient Ireland from Prehistory to the Middle Ages*, where his text accompanies the magnificent photographs of Jacqueline O'Brien, (London, 1996).
78. Thomas Mann, *Dr. Faustus* (New York: Alfred A. Knopf, 1948), p. 268.
79. Teilhard de Chardin, *Le Milieu Divin* (Penguin, 1963), pp. 77-8.